The Guided Reading Classroom

How to Keep ALL Students Working Constructively

Nancy L. Witherell

HEINEMANN
Portsmouth, NH

Heinemann
A division of Reed Elsevier Inc.
361 Hanover Street
Portsmouth, NH 03801–3912
www.heinemann.com

Offices and agents throughout the world

Library of Congress Cataloging-in-Publication Data
Witherell, Nancy L.
    The guided reading classroom : how to keep all students working constructively / Nancy L. Witherell.
        p. cm.
    Includes bibliographical references and index.
    ISBN-13: 978-0-325-00924-7 (alk. paper)
    ISBN-10: 0-325-00924-4
1. Guided reading. 2. Group reading. I. Title.
    LB1050.377.W58 2007
    372.41'62—dc22   2006103061

Editor: Kate Montgomery
Production editor: Sonja S. Chapman
Cover design: Jenny Jensen Greenleaf
Compositor: Tom Allen, Pear Graphic Design
Manufacturing: Steve Bernier

Printed in the United States of America on acid-free paper
11 10 09 08 07 ML 1 2 3 4 5

For their support, I send love and thanks to my husband, Peter W. Witherell,
and my friend, Mary C. McMackin.

CONTENTS

Guided reading has always been one of my favorite reading contexts. Working with guided reading groups allows a teacher to know each child so much more than in a whole-class setting. In guided reading groups students and teachers talk to each other. Opinions are given. Thoughts and connections are made. Teachers are given a close-up snapshot of individual students. Being successful in guided reading is a goal worth attaining. My goal for this book is to help teachers make a smooth transition when implementing guided reading in their classrooms.

This book contains assumptions. It assumes that the reader has background knowledge on guided reading, can name the "gurus" (such as Fountas and Pinnell), and can give a reasonable explanation of what guided reading entails. The purpose of this book is to help teachers who are having difficulty putting guided reading into place. The readers of this book will be at different places on the continuum to what they consider an okay place to be with guided reading and that is okay because the comfort zone of the teacher, when implementing and continuing guided reading, is so important. When we are not comfortable we get frustrated. We get cranky. We quit.

We can't quit. Guided reading, which goes hand in hand with leveled groups, supported reading, and differentiated instruction, is too important. In small-group instruction the students have more contact with the teacher. Student participation is higher. The ratio of students to teacher goes down to one third or one fourth of the whole class. Students who sit quietly in the whole-class context are noticed more in smaller guided reading groups. They get to talk; the teacher listens.

Through that listening instructional decisions are made. Teachers naturally begin to ask themselves questions as children interact in the group. Do they understand? If not, what is the interference? What's the complication?

What can I do to help? What do I do next? That last question is key. It is where assessment begins to guide instruction, where children begin to learn, where we need to be, and where we can go with guided reading.

ACKNOWLEDGMENTS

I would like to thank Helen Collis, Jaime Reid, and Debra Waterman, teachers of Burnell Elementary School and friends of mine, for letting me into their classrooms to teach, observe, and learn. Jaime, an outstanding and retiring educator, will be missed. I thank Gloria Stanton, the principal of the Burnell Elementary School, for allowing us the freedom to explore. Also, my appreciation goes to Mary Tanguay, for so kindly scanning items needed in this book.

My appreciation goes to Ronnie Zusman, a friend and former teacher, for her creativity and attention to detail as she shared long-term project ideas with me.

I would be remiss if I didn't thank my Heinemann editors Kerry Herlihy and Kate Montgomery: Kerry, for reading too many times, giving wonderful suggestions, and always offering encouragement, and Kate, who was there from the beginning, for her faith and support in this project.

And finally, I would like to thank my sister, Genie Stonesifer, who, as we worked together to help Mom, would simply say, "Go write."

CHAPTER 1

Why Guided Reading Fits into a Comprehensive Language Arts Program

Walking into Mrs. Keily's fourth-grade classroom, we see Noah and Aaron talking excitedly over the poster they are creating. When questioned, we find they are thrilled because they have just discovered that frogs can be red. Not only that, but Aaron searched online and found one for sale for six dollars! They think it would be dangerously cool to own a poisonous frog. The boys are discussing putting a for sale sign next to the red frog they are drawing and including the fact that the frog was from South America.

Other students around the room are engaged and at various stages of research and design for their amphibian posters. Some students are partner reading assigned text, and we noticed one child ask her partner what a word meant. The answer is clear enough, and they continue reading. They know that after reading they are to work independently at their desk. Time is important.

The teacher is in a corner of the room, working with a group and pointing out different text features as the students read. Mrs. Keily asks students to read the caption under the picture and is quickly able to point to the caption for Jesse as he begins to read the first paragraph instead. Mrs. Keily then asks students to read the caption under the next picture, and students read together. She then has students tell each other what a caption is, and she ends this part of the lesson by having the group give a definition.

Walking into Mrs. Keily's classroom is a learning adventure, where things are happening, children are engaged, and learning is the optimal point. Guided reading does that. Managing the guided reading classroom effectively enables teachers to take their students as far as possible in their reading. This book will help you do that.

What Happens in Whole Class Reading?

In contrast to Mrs. Keily's room, let's take a look at a third-grade class using whole-class reading. The teacher, Mr. Belwick, is wonderful, very conscientious and follows the anthology directions to the point. He uses all the suggestions mentioned under "Meeting Individual Differences" in bold on the sides of the teacher's manual. But he knows it is not working. He has AJ, who speeds through the book twice as fast as most students in class, and sure enough, he discusses the section well and goes through the follow-up work with flying colors. Then there is Sarah, who reads at reasonable speed, and for the most part does well. Sometimes, Sarah gives an unsupported answer to an open-ended question or responds to independent work incorrectly. Yet, after some discussion, she's fine. Stacey, on the other hand, never seems to completely read the selection by the time all of the others have finished. Mr. Belwick gives as much time as he can, but there are other subjects in the day, and the rest of the class is waiting for the postreading discussion. So, Stacey, for the most part, never really reads the ending. She listens to what the other students have to say and rarely raises her hand to be included in the discussion. Her written and oral responses are rarely on track even when Mr. Belwick has sat with Stacey and scaffolded her learning by reading some of the text to her.

This scenario happens every day in some classrooms. It is so different from what we saw happening in Mrs. Keily's room. AJ, Sarah, and Stacey are all reading from the same book. Not only are they on different reading levels but they also have different needs. No matter how much Mr. Belwick strives to meet all of their needs within the context of using the same-leveled book, it is not going to happen. Unless some outside influences occur, no matter how well-intended Mr. Belwick's instruction is, Stacey will not show optimal learning and AJ may not either. AJ will be reading at the independent level and he will most likely show progress in reading, although this learning community does not challenge him. AJ has managed to become an above-grade-level reader in spite of the system. Sarah will do fine; in some ways she is the lucky one. The anthology is at Sarah's instructional reading level, and she is advancing in reading. Sometimes it is a struggle because she is not at her independent level and the text can be confusing to her, but that is part of going forward. On the other hand, Stacey, unknown to Mr. Belwick, will spend her full year reading frustration-level material. In science and social studies it will be worse because there is less scaffolding in the areas where the material is more difficult for her. Stacey already knows she's a poor reader. She can't answer any questions right, her written work is always wrong, and even though Mr. Belwick helps her, she just doesn't get some things. She knows she is stupid, but it doesn't matter because she hates reading anyway.

Why Guided Reading?

We need guided reading groups for the AJs and Staceys of this world, and in some classrooms this may include a large percentage of the classroom population. According to McCardle and Chhabra (2004) more than one third of fourth graders cannot read simple books. In contrast, Allington (2001) states that research is pointing to high level of reading achievements but that particular groups of students lag behind their peers. These are students whose parents are not high school graduates, students of low income, students of younger-aged mothers, and minority students. In addition, taking into consideration that English language learners are the fastest growing group in U.S. schools today (Vardell, Hadaway, and Young, 2006) the need for "just right" group instruction intensifies.

For optimal learning even Sarah, who is in the just right–level book, would also benefit from small-group instruction. If leveled reading groups are not in place, students in many classrooms use as their main reading textbooks that are at their independent or frustration level. The students continue getting taught (but are not necessarily learning) for the whole school year—or more—using an inappropriate book. Obviously students deserve to be taught reading with material and curriculum that is at their instructional level or need.

Guided Reading in a Nutshell

Guided reading allows teachers to support readers' strategic development as they progress into increasingly difficult text (Fountas and Pinnell 1996). The teacher offers small-group instruction to children with similar needs and on a similar level in reading. The goal is to aid students in their journey to becoming independent, strategic readers. Students need the opportunity to repeatedly read instructional-level texts (Tyner and Green 2005). The teacher differentiates instruction by bringing together homogenous readers in a small-group setting where specific skills and strategies can be taught as needed by these students. Guiding reading allows both teachers and students to be the best they can be.

Guided reading allows teachers to work in small groups while the rest of the class is engaged in independent or collaborative learning activities.

Guided reading assumes that children are reading text at their instructional level. It is recommended that guided reading groups be no more than six in size, although I have worked successfully with a larger number in above-grade-level groups. Fountas and Pinnell (1996) offer wonderful explanations about what should happen in a guided reading lesson. According to these authors, the purpose of the teacher in these lessons is to provide a frame for meaning for the students. The teacher introduces the text and helps the children make connections. Children silently read a short section of the text, or in some cases a short book, and then the group discusses the material. The teacher is with the group to clarify any points or correct any misunderstandings. After (or sometimes before) the reading is an optimum time to give explanations on what good readers need to understand, such as text features, idiomatic phrases within the text, or text structure.

Fountas and Pinnell (1996) offer essential elements of guided reading for before, during, and after the reading. In prereading instruction they suggest teachers introduce the story and perhaps some text features and leave questions for the reader to consider while reading. During the reading the teacher observes, confirms, interacts with some individuals, and takes observation notes. Postreading instruction includes the story discussion with personal responses, clarification or teaching of learning points, and perhaps an extension. The lesson plan ideas offered in this book include more than the Fountas and Pinnell model, but because the guided reading time is limited, it is imperative that teachers focus on students' need. Once the guided reading lesson is done, the group is sent back to their seats to work independently of the teacher. This may be a response to the story or some other literacy activity, which will be elaborated on in this book.

How Does This Happen?

Organization and planning are the keys to successful implementation of guided reading. Guided reading can be planning intensive, but the rewards are well worth the effort. When teachers discuss their guided reading classrooms, two main benefits seem to emerge: the joy of working with children at their own level and having the opportunity to know each child better. When a teacher works with a group of six, for that twenty- or thirty-minute time period, there is a miniclassroom of one teacher and six students. Everyone gets noticed, a high majority feel comfortable enough to participate, even children who may not in a large-class setting, and teachers can evaluate progress more readily.

The concept of "doing more with less" not only eases the planning but also allows for the repetition needed by the students to thoroughly take ownership of material. We can do more with less in a variety of ways and many samples will be discussed in the following chapters. For example, in a word study group the teacher is working with contractions and has made a matching game for students to play. She has designed her group lesson around the gradual release of responsibility model. In this game students must match eight contractions with the whole words from which they are derived. First, the teacher explains contractions and shows some examples in books. Then she teaches the eight that she plans to reinforce with the game cards. She then passes out to the group the game cards with the contraction words. Next, the teacher holds up the two whole words one at a time for each contraction. She then has the student with the matching contraction give her the card. Once this is finished, she gives a set of matching cards to partners in the group and they show they can match these correctly. For follow-up work the students are told to play a game of concentration with the cards. They must put the cards together in pairs when they have completed their game so the teacher can check them. Then the students must go back to their reading and write the sentence in which the contraction is found. Underneath the sentence they must write the two words that form the contraction. This may seem like an overkill, but in reality it is not. Let's look at the lesson: There was direct instruction and an interactive gamelike activity between the students and the teacher. Then there was a collaborative, and thereby a social, activity in matching the words with the contractions. When the students left the group to do their follow-up, it was done in a fun, interactive way. Finally, going back into the book, writing the contraction in context, and matching this with the two words solidifies the learning. An overkill? There is a reason why we teach contractions in grades 1, 2, 3, 4, and sometimes 5. For some students this is a strong instructional approach enabling them to grasp the material. The teacher has made a set of games that have been well used and can then be placed in a word study center, hence, more with less.

Not only has the teacher done more with less, but also the curriculum has been kept flowing. The gradual release of responsibility model has been used in the instruction. The lesson went from all teacher direction to guided practice to independent work with the sentences. The lesson kept the curriculum flowing as it continued on with reinforcing the contractions and brought these back into the book.

Guided Reading Addresses Individual Instructional Needs

In Mr. Belwick's example Sarah is doing fine, but sometimes she struggles. It appears Sarah is being taught at her instructional level in reading but sometimes shows the "pain" in the gain. When we discuss students' individual instructional needs, we are looking for those times when students' needs do not match the rest of their peers. In Sarah's case, it is important that the teacher recognize what the struggle is and do some quick remediation. Sarah is on grade level; we want to help her progress and not allow her to slip behind. If Sarah has problems answering open-ended questions, it may be that Sarah needs some comprehension strategies. She may need to use the "look back" strategy to support answers or she may need direct instruction on how to "read between the lines."

Stacey, although on a different instructional level, could be struggling with the same problem. The solution is to group Stacey and Sarah (and other students identified with this need) and offer a minilesson or series of minilessons to address this area of concern. Although Sarah and Stacy are on different reading levels, in this instance they have the same need: strategies that can aid them in making inferences. This flexibility in grouping helps all students.

When using flexible grouping Mr. Belwick would model and have this strategy group apply techniques to aid in comprehension. He would use a common text that these students can all read with ease, enabling the focus to be on the strategy instruction. Once improvement is seen, this group will be disbanded and another instructional need group formed. In some ways, the skill and strategy grouping is a "damage control" method. We would hope that our minilessons and guided reading group instruction would be enough to keep students on pace with the expected learning. Unfortunately, we don't live in an ideal world. We need flexible grouping in both instructional-level groups and skills or strategy grouping and must use formative assessment to keep students at an optimal learning pace.

Formative assessment is as it sounds. It is what effective teachers do every day in their classrooms. The term *formative assessment* puts a name on something teachers have been doing since the beginning of time. When using formative assessment, teachers informally assess students daily on their progress and use this knowledge to guide their daily instruction. For example, if Jerome is making the letter *B* look more like the letter *P*, the teacher takes thirty seconds to model for Jerome and checks Jerome's understanding of the letter formation. If Laura can't answer simple what and when questions in which the answers are explicitly stated in the book, the teacher stops and models the look back strategy, and then asks another question to see if Laura can use this strategy. This informal assessment directs the teacher to the next step in the child's learning. The current trend for accountability has upped the ante and the term *forma-*

tive assessment used in educational circles today implies that the formative assessment is both systematic and often recorded to account for growth.

Guided Reading Keeps Students at Their Optimal Learning Pace

There is irony in that students may need to sometimes leave their comfort zones to show growth, and to some educators of young children, this is also uncomfortable. A few years back a poster promoting reading was very popular in school classrooms. It stated, "To become a better reader: read, read, read, read, read, read, read, read, read, and read." We know that helps, but in reality for students to become better readers they must read material that is challenging for them in order to increase both their reading abilities and cognition skills. When children (and adults for that matter) read material that is challenging, there may be some discomfort. Think of the times in your own learning when you have been assigned a text that has taxed your brain. You can read the words with comfort, but there is an anxiety in deciphering the author's message. Once you have formed an understanding of the text, the result is a proud relief. For children we can scaffold their learning so as they stretch their capabilities, we can ease the pain in their gain and actually make learning fun!

The gradual release of responsibility model (Pearson and Gallagher 1983) gives teachers an instructional model that ensures that students learn with little anxiety and simultaneously uses formative assessment to verify that correct learning is taking place. The gradual release of responsibility model begins with the teacher having full responsibility for the learning. The teacher may use explicit instruction or model the new material. Then he gradually releases the responsibility of the task and the learning over to the student (see Figure 1–1).

Shared reading, when followed with individual reading, offers a perfect example of the gradual release of responsibility model. The lesson may take place over several days, but the responsibility of the reading is eventually handed over to the students. Initially the teacher working with a small group reads the big book to the students. As the teacher reads, she stops and checks understanding, clarifying points that are not clear. Students are given time to question and to make connections to their own lives. Then the teacher and the children read together, using different techniques. For instance, the students may choral read along with the teacher; the teacher may read orally,

Figure 1–1. *Responsibility Is Gradually Released to the Student*

All Teacher	Guided Practice	All Student
Instruction begins with the teacher. Inductively or explicitly the teacher instructs students on the content. The responsibility belongs to the teacher.	The teacher carefully takes students through the new learning. Initially the teacher may model as the students practice. Then students work individually, in small groups, or with partners as the teacher observes and aids in the practice. Guided practice is the joint responsibility of both the teacher and student. Teacher guidance is still needed.	At this point the student can successfully complete the task independently. The teacher's role is to observe and assess.

The gradual release of responsibility model of instruction, adapted from P. D. Pearson and M. C. Gallagher, "The Instruction of Reading Comprehension." *Contemporary Educational Psychology* 8:314–44, 1983.

with students reading along silently with specific parts designated for choral reading; or the teacher may work with story words that are new to the group by manipulating their order on a chart. In all of this the teacher has the main responsibility. Once the teacher assesses that students may successfully read with less help, she then gives the group more responsibility but continues to guide their practice. At this point the teacher may pair students with smaller-size versions of the big book and walk around the reading table listening as partners read to each other. Eventually with guided practice, students will be able to read this book independently and they will be given time to do this during their independent work time. Hence the responsibility of the reading has gone from all teacher responsibility to that of the student. In the meantime, students in the class who no longer are dependent upon shared reading experiences have been partner reading and responding to a higher-leveled text.

How Teachers Can Use This Book

This book can be approached in different ways. It has been organized to give the theory, research-based information, and an overview of different components of the guided reading program; then examples of classroom application are offered, followed by a variety of ideas that can be used in any classroom. You may decide to read the book in its entirety to capture ideas and information that will be useful in your classroom. Or, if you know you hate centers, you may skip reading that section, although I would implore you to read the overview and rationale! This book is chock-full of ideas to help you create an engaging and motivating guided reading classroom.

In Conclusion

Guided reading allows for much more than instructional-level grouping. Students are given assigned tasks that are engaging and challenging enough to compel them to learn. It is driven by formative assessment and results in student progress.

CHAPTER 2

Organizing Group and Independent Activity Time

How Does Guided Reading Fit into a Comprehensive Language Arts Block?

The biggest problem classroom teachers mention when implementing guided reading is not what to do with the reading groups, but how to fit *everything* into their language arts block. What should the language arts block contain and where should it go? Guided reading fits, but the fit is different in each classroom. Fountas and Pinnell (1996) promote guided reading within a balanced literacy program, explaining that guided reading is only one component of the whole program. Students meet with guided reading groups from ten to thirty minutes and spend a great portion of their day in other literacy-rich instruction and activities.

The language arts block itself can be divided in shorter time chunks so other components of the literacy curriculum can be pursued. One component, minilessons, are often used to begin the language arts block. Teachers use this time to introduce or reinforce important aspects of literacy, for instance, lessons to improve writing or reinforce phonics skills. Students need independent work time to be available for reader responses, projects, or centers.

Why Small-Group Instruction?

Drew contributes so much to our discussions. At the beginning of the term, he was hesitant and unsure of himself as he answered questions. I'm sure he knew his answers were weak. In the reading group, I began to have students find and read support for their answers. After a few days of asking for, showing, and discussing how a sentence or a word could support an answer, I could almost see Drew having an "aha" moment. His answers began to make more sense, and he would actually say that he had found support for his answer! If I didn't have my class in reading groups, I would never have noticed this.

Comments like this come often from teachers of guided reading. Guided reading has become synonymous with small group instruction, which according to Fountas and Pinnell (1996) should include not just guided reading groups but also flexible groups for specific skills or strategies. Teaching with small groups allows teachers to get to know their students' thinking. Making small-group instruction possible takes organizational skill and a great amount of preplanning, like teaching in general. The challenge is to keep the rest of the class not only engaged in learning but progressing. If teachers are working with reading groups for over an hour each day, the other students must utilize this time effectively. Teachers need to design connecting, yet motivating tasks for students to do with minimal teacher assistance and yet remain challenged. Is it a wonder we are not sure what to do with the rest of the class?

The purpose of this chapter is to help teachers decide an organizational pattern that allows for class, group, and individual time. The organizational structures shared here include blocks of time for guided reading groups, centers, long-term projects, and reading response (independent work). The teacher needs to find the grouping pattern that works for his own purposes and goals in the classroom. This depends upon a number of factors such as room size, materials available, number of leveled reading groups, and so on. The two top priorities should be the needs of the students and the comfort of the teacher.

How to Begin?

As the teacher incorporates guided reading and leveled groups into the classroom, time must be spent "setting up for success." It may be that in the first week of guided reading, no guided reading groups meet. If classes are not conditioned to working in centers or being responsible for their own independent work time, the teacher may need to be available for a week or two until student expectations have been established.

Mrs. Shapiro knows that guided reading would greatly improve her students' reading performance. Mrs. Shapiro enjoys her very active class of

Figure 2–1. *Grouping Model 1*

	Group A	**Group B**	**Group C**
9:00–9:30	Guided reading time	Center time	Reading response time
9:30–10:00	Reading response time	Guided reading time	Center time
10:00-10:30	Center time	Reading response time	Guided reading time

Figure 2–2. *Grouping Model 2, No Centers*

	Group A	**Group B**	**Group C**
9:00–9:30	Guided reading time	Project time	Reading response time
9:30–10:00	Reading response time	Guided reading time	Project time
10:00-10:30	Project time	Reading response time	Guided reading time

twenty-two students. Assessments indicate that students can be placed in three differently leveled instruction groups. Mrs. Shapiro looks at the two models that show the organizational pattern for meeting three groups in a guided reading classroom (Figures 2–1 and Figure 2–2).

Mrs. Shapiro had considered going without centers and allowing project time, but she loves centers. She decides to try the guided reading/center/reading response organizational pattern (Figure 2–1). She designs and prepares five center areas in her classroom: a computer station, a writing center, reading area, word study center, and listening center. She is excited about the ideas and materials she has gathered for her centers; she feels they will work well and do not require hours of prep. Mrs. Shapiro is uncomfortable just dividing the groups into three time slots and telling them what to do. She wants to avoid disaster. She decides to implement the guided reading organization pattern in stages. The organizational structures Mrs. Shapiro will include are:

- blocks of time for guided reading groups

- flex time for organization smoothness

- centers

- short-term projects

- minilessons

On the first day, Mrs. Shapiro explains the tasks and choices at each center. She models when necessary and clearly states the student behavior expectations at each center and the classroom system for handing in center work.

On the second day, after doing reading and reading response activities with the whole class as a minilesson, Mrs. Shapiro declares it is center time for everyone. She explains the "center board," which tells the students which center they are assigned to for the day (see Figure 2–3). Three to five students will be at each center (just for the training period will the center groups be this large). She then reminds students they are to walk quietly to their assigned center and begin their center work. Mrs. Shapiro guides the students at the various centers. Initially she allows students fifteen minutes of center time and makes sure they are following her expectations. Prior to students returning to their seats, she explains again how they are to handle

Figure 2–3. *Center Board (When and Where Students Are to Be)*

	Computer Station	Writing Center	Reading Area	Word Study Center	Listening Center
9:00–9:20	Sarah B. Anna	Luke	Jose	Belinda	Juan Joey
9:30–9:50	Jonathan Julia	Victoria Cassandra	Kyle	Tyler	Sadie Emily
10:00–10:20	Julieta	Antonio Mikey	Ava	Sarah H.	Matthew Marina

Student names need to be mobile. You can purchase the flat little wooden shape cutouts of male and female figures. You can then put the students' names on their gender "doll" and put magnetic tape on back. In this classroom, the center board was taped to a file cabinet and the magnetic figures moved easily. The student names could be placed in their center for the day and changed with ease.

the completed and incomplete work. Finally, Mrs. Shapiro holds a "debriefing" with her students. They discuss what went well during center time and what didn't, once again reviewing classroom expectations. After three days of guiding students through center time, Mrs. Shapiro is comfortable with the student center work habits.

On the fifth day, Mrs. Shapiro meets with the guided reading groups. She teaches a minilesson on contractions. One group goes to centers, one group does the minilesson follow-up and the third group meets with her. On the sixth and seventh days Mrs. Shapiro meets with the other two guided reading groups for one time slot. The students have now tried everything needed to succeed in the organizational pattern. Mrs. Shapiro feels she and her class are ready for three guided reading groups to meet on a daily or near daily basis. She has set up her class for a successful transition to leveled reading groups.

When setting up her reading group meeting times, Mrs. Shapiro has purposely left ten minutes between group times. This, especially as she begins guided reading, allows her to manipulate the time. She can use the ten minutes for "housekeeping" with the class as they change activities. She can keep the guided reading group with her longer, or she can meet with children at their seat doing reader responses. She may want to talk to one group just for five minutes prior to giving them their assigned task for the reader response time. She may also use this time to help individual students in a "minitutorial" fashion.

An Alternative Approach to Guided Reading Organization

On the other hand, Mr. Salvo, a fifth-grade teacher, has a class of twenty-seven students. He hates centers, with the exception perhaps of a computer station, but he uses computers often with his students for writing. He has assessed his students and feels that he can divide the class into four instructional-level groups, the approximate grade levels being grades 3, 4, 5 and 7. Mr. Salvo has decided to use a grouping model that allows for flexibility. His reading block is about ninety-five minutes long. He also has to place his minilesson within that time limit. Mr. Salvo knows he cannot meet with four different groups each day. He feels comfortable not meeting with each group every day, as long as he guides students' reader response and project time. Mr. Salvo will be using a flexible grouping model (Figure 2–4).

Because Mr. Salvo has four groups he will be meeting with group A (grade 3 readers) daily. He will be meeting with group B (grade 4–level read-

Figure 2-4. *Grouping Model 3, No Centers*

Whole class (begins each day)

	Group A	Group B	Group C
Day 1	Guided reading Reading response	Reading response Guided reading	Reading response Project time
Day 2	Guided reading Reading response	Reading response Project time	(or group D) Project time Guided reading
Day 3	Project time Guided reading	Guided reading Reading response	Reading response Project time
Day 4	Reading response Guided reading	(or group D) Project time Guided reading	Guided reading Project time

Figure 2-5. *Daily Scheduling*

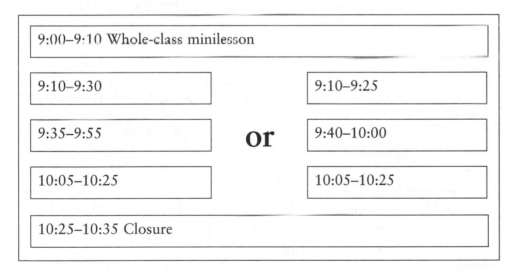

9:00–9:10 Whole-class minilesson

9:10–9:30   9:10–9:25

9:35–9:55   **or**   9:40–10:00

10:05–10:25   10:05–10:25

10:25–10:35 Closure

ers) four out of five days. He will be meeting with group C (grade 5 instructional level) three days a week, and finally, group D (grade 7 instructional level) just twice a week. He has weighted his meeting times to the needs of his students. Mr. Salvo has set up his daily schedule (see Figure 2–5), so he can have time before class, between groups, and at the end. On the days that

Mr. Salvo does not meet with a group, they get expanded reading response or project time.

Because Mr. Salvo meets with his grade 3 instructional-level group daily, sometimes he decides to shorten the group time. He is delighted he can do this because it gives him a little more time to help other groups doing independent work or to have minitutorials with individual students. Mr. Shapiro feels that it is very important to begin and end the reading time as a class community. Today, he chooses to use the closure time to read more of "A Series of Unfortunate Events." He has been reading that daily after lunch, but the students are really into the Baudelaire orphans' unfortunate events, and they have asked him to read more. Because during their project time students are writing their own unfortunate events chapters, Mr. Salvo feels that this extra read-aloud might help his students. He is excited as the students have wonderful ideas, but he sees the need to help them gain stronger writing voices.

Depending on the diverse needs in the classroom, as in Mr. Salvo's class, sometimes more than three instructional levels are needed. Teachers need to be cognizant that too many leveled groups may mean that no one gets enough instructional time to allow optimal growth for any of the students. Figure 2–6 shows another four-group workable model. This model includes teacher time, center time, reading response time, and project time. This model can be adjusted to three groups, allowing the teacher time to work

Figure 2–6. *Grouping Model 4*

	Group A	Group B	Group C	Group D
9:00–9:20	Guided reading time	Center time	Project time	Reading response time
9:25–9:45	Reading response time	Guided reading time	Center time	Project time
9:50–10:10	Project time	Reading response time	Guided reading time	Center time
10:15–10:35	Center time	Project time	Reading response time	Guided reading time

with individual students, to gather together flexible skills groups, or for individual assessment. For instance, a teacher could meet with a group from 9:00 to 9:20, 9:25 to 9:45, and 10:15 to 10:35. This will allow the teacher to meet with skills groups, pairs, or individuals from 9:50 to 10:10. Or a teacher could decide to meet with groups the first three time slots (9:00 to 9:20, 9:25 to 9:45, 9:50 to 10:10), freeing the last twenty-five minutes. This last time slot can be used to check individual papers or perform running records, retellings, and other types of formative assessments. This is what makes guided reading so exciting: being able to choose what works best for the teacher and the class!

Which Is Right for Me?

As a teacher begins her journey into guided reading, a great amount of thought must go into the organization of the classroom. In some ways it is like buying a new car. Before going to a dealer you have narrowed down some choices, perhaps a jeep, minivan, or convertible. When you sit behind the wheel, you begin to judge if this is the car for you. Then there is the test-drive. Is it really what you want? Are you comfortable here? In choosing your organizational model you probably have an idea of which one you want to test-drive. Now it's time to get behind the wheel. That's when the excitement begins!

CHAPTER 3

Minilessons: Preparing for Independent Success

What Are Minilessons?

Minilessons are purposeful, short lessons that focus on a slice of content or a particular skill or strategy. According to Fountas and Pinnell (1996) the minilesson provides a short, focused lesson. Often, these lessons center on an area of the curriculum that teachers have observed as a weakness for the students. It is through minilessons that teachers prepare students to be successful during their independent work or guided reading activities. The minilesson topic often comes from teacher observation during reading groups or reader response evaluations. As we use assessment to guide instruction, we use minilessons to keep that instruction focused and to prepare the students to apply their learning. For instance, if students are reading leveled expository books, the teacher can use the minilesson time to explain the purpose of the bold print or captions and then have students work with these during their reading groups. Or the minilesson could focus on the need for interesting and important facts in preparation for summary writing, and students will categorize and discuss interesting and important facts during their reading group time as reinforcement.

Usually lasting five to ten minutes, a minilesson can be used for a variety of purposes, to teach a new strategy or skill, to reinforce learning, to model, to reteach when needed, or to explain housekeeping procedures. The short time frame adds to the effectiveness of the lesson by forcing the lesson topic to be narrow and the lesson to be focused. This limits the amount of material that can be included, and for many students the "downsized" information enables them to have a greater chance of absorbing what is being taught.

As mentioned previously, minilessons can be directly connected to the texts children are using for their guided reading lessons. Because children are reading different books at different levels, it may seem more difficult to give the whole class a common minilesson. In reality, it's not. Books have a number of commonalities, whether they are narrative or expository. So, the minilesson may extend to the whole class, or additionally, a small part of the guided reading time for one group. If you have a group of students who are having difficulty using context clues, using a cloze procedure in a minilesson might be advantageous for this group. Or if students are learning story elements, a whole-class minilesson on story mapping might be appropriate.

Minilessons are organized to scaffold and model students' independent tasks. A minilesson usually targets a piece of the day's curriculum but can be built upon to expand learning. Sometimes, it may take a number of minilessons to reach the targeted goal. Minilessons should be designed to include modeling and guided practice, leading eventually to independent practice. The teaching points need to be concise, and clear. The following scenario shows a series of focused minilessons. Mrs. Weld is preparing her class to effectively read expository texts. This is reinforced in their guided reading groups.

What Are Minilessons Like?

Ms. Weld's focus is to teach her students how to use bold-faced type to preview the text. In the first minilesson Ms. Weld uses the overhead to show the whole class what this strategy looks like. She uses an example from a children's magazine and chooses a one-page article on panda bears. Ms. Weld puts the page on the overhead and shows the students how the bold-faced print gives her the gist of what the article says about bears. As she reads the bold-faced print, Ms. Weld does a think-aloud. She reads the bold-faced type "Gourmet Meals for Pandas" and says, "Ah, this part is going to tell me what pandas really like to eat." She then reads the bold-faced print "Panda's Habitat." She says, "Gee, *habitat* means where an animal lives, so the author must be going to tell me where pandas live." And finally she reads the bold-faced type "On the Endangered List" and says, "Wow, I didn't know it, but pandas must be an endangered species. Now, I know an endangered species means that the animals are dying out. I would hate to see panda bears disappear." Ms. Weld then explains that by reading the bold-faced print she has a pretty good idea what the article is going to be about, and she is curious to read it. She also mentions that by previewing she will most likely have a better understanding when reading the entire article.

Ms. Weld has now modeled a small part of previewing expository text. She knows there is more. Students must still learn to look at captions and to read charts. She chose this article because of its simplicity. After modeling this simple preview Ms. Weld tells the students to notice the bold-faced print in books as they read. They are not yet ready to successfully preview, and Ms. Weld does not want to spend more time on today's minilesson.

The next day, Ms. Weld has a one-page article on skiing. She guides the lesson as she asks the students to read the bold-faced print and share their thinking of what the article might be about as they read. After previewing the bold-faced print, she asks students if they are curious about anything the bold-faced print has mentioned. She once again explains that reading the bold-faced print helps readers with comprehension in that readers are able to make a map in their head about the article's topic. Ms. Weld will assign this article to be read during independent time because she wants the students to carry over this strategy into independent learning.

The children, according to Ms. Weld's observations, are ready to practice this skill. During the guided reading lesson she partners students to preview three to four pages of the expository text. She walks around the group to check that partners are previewing the bold-faced type and not partner reading the book. Once the group has previewed, the students give Ms. Weld ideas on what they will be reading. Ms. Weld has made a successful beginning with previewing techniques. She is confident that students using this strategy will have a higher comprehension and retain more information from their readings.

The previous scenario shows how narrow the topic of a minilesson tends to be. Next, Ms. Weld could continue on with previewing by adding graphs, tables, and charts to the text. This would be simplified, however, if how to read a graph, table, or chart were taught in a math lesson. Then Ms. Weld could concentrate on adding these items to the "what to preview list" and the students will have already accomplished the skill of gathering information from these text features.

How Do You Organize Minilessons?

It is hard for some teachers to understand that there is almost no "approach to the lesson" in the minilesson format. Traditionally, classroom lessons usually include: the outcome, materials, approach, procedures, and culmination. These components have proven to be effective in helping teachers enable students to grasp new material and content. The minilesson has a different purpose than the more traditional and fact-laden classroom lesson. It may be that the focus is narrow, a new instructional strategy is being used, material is being reinforced, or previously taught material is being extended. Often, the most effective minilessons are designed around the content and instructional needs of the students' task during their independent work time. This, of course, stems from what is being taught in the guided reading groups.

Minilesson plans should focus on the following components: the outcomes, materials, and procedures. The plan should answer these questions: What are you teaching? With what? And how are you going to teach it? In keeping with the short minilessons, plans, whether written or internalized, should also be short!

Ms. Weld's first minilesson on previewing would look like this:

Focus

Previewing text: Bold-faced print.

Outcomes

Students should recognize that expository text can be previewed by reading the bold-faced print.

Materials

Magazine article on pandas, overhead of article.

Procedure

Use overhead to show students the bold-faced print. Model previewing by using a think-aloud.

The plan can be written on a copy of the format sheet (see Appendix 3–1) or an index card can be used. Ms. Weld's second minilesson plan would look like this:

Focus

Previewing text: Bold-faced print.

Outcomes

Students should recognize that to preview expository text, they should read the bold-faced print, and that this strategy helps with comprehension and making a "map" in their minds.

Materials

One page of article on skiing copied for each student.

Procedure

Have volunteers read bold-faced print. Have students discuss each one as it is read. Discuss how bold-faced print helps us see what the article will be about, and aids in comprehension and remembering details. Ask students what they think they will learn by reading the article. (The article will be read during independent time.)

When looking over the two minilessons, notice the narrow focus and how the second lesson builds on the first. Because of the minilessons' short duration there is no time to waste, but a fast-paced lesson may be confusing. Fountas and Pinnell (2001) suggest that the central understanding of the minilesson be stated in one clear thought. It is important to keep the lesson's outcome in mind and limit the amount of material to be covered. For many topics it is a matter of breaking the strategy or skill into sections or "chunking" the material. For example, in letter writing, one minilesson could simply center on how to write the heading in a letter.

Assessing the Minilesson

Often when I am cleaning up from some volunteer activity, be it a literacy event, parent group activity, or church social, I will say, "It's not over till it's over." Just because the activity has ended, until everything is put away and things are in their proper place the job is not done. Even then we have a little more work to do. We assess our own actions by asking, How did the activity go? Would we do the same next time? Because minilessons are such an important structure to explicit teaching in the guided reading classroom, we must constantly assess the results of this instruction.

The teaching of the minilesson does not make a teacher's job complete. It is not over until the students have been assessed as having successfully reached the intended outcomes. This could be through observation of students, evaluation of tasks, or observing in some way an acceptable level of competence. As we observe students for their understanding, we intuitively begin to reflect on the lesson. How did the activity go? Would we do it the same the next time? If the students are not "getting it," what needs to be different? If one or two students need help, what can we do? In this way, it's not over till it's over.

For instance, Mrs. Binder teaches a minilesson on using word parts to figure out word meaning. One guided reading group has the words *improbable* and *territory* in their book. During her lesson Mrs. Binder focuses on these two words to assess and reinforce students' learning from the minilesson. Students remember that the prefix *im* means *not*, and they know the word *probably*, so they are able discern the gist of the word *improbable*. When working with *territory*, Mrs. Binder discovers the students have no background to decipher the word meaning. She talks about *terra* being a Latin root meaning *earth* or *land* prior to discussing the definition of *territory*. Mrs. Binder asks students if they know any words that have *ter* or *terra* in them, the response includes *terrarium* and an *ATV* (all terrain vehicle). From this guided reading discussion, Mrs. Binder makes a mental note to do a few minilessons on appropriate Latin and Greek roots.

Concluding Thoughts

The most effective minilessons teach something that will be seen again within the reading and/or writing block. They are the starting points for a more comprehensive learning experience. What begins in a minilesson may appear again during any time of the school day. So, in reality the teacher will be assessing over and over again the success of the lesson. Through careful observation a teacher will glean any piece of the learning that must be clarified. Minilessons that connect to the text being read often reappear in the prereading, during reading, and/or postreading section of a reading lesson, which emphasizes the importance of the minilesson. The next few chapters offer ideas to effectively connect minilessons to a variety of books.

Lesson Plan Format

Date _____   Group _____

Focus
Outcomes
Materials
Procedure

©2007 by Nancy L. Witherell from *The Guided Reading Classroom*. Portsmouth, NH: Heinemann.

CHAPTER 4

How to Structure Independent Activities Throughout the Reading Lesson

Reading lessons, like all well-written lessons, have three main sections, the approach: the body, and the culmination. In reading jargon, this becomes *prereading*, *during reading*, and *postreading*. Breaking a lesson into multiple components allows for scaffolding, which helps to ensure that our students gain understanding by supporting the learning. Each section of the lesson offers components that aid and scaffold students in their understanding. This differs from minilessons, as the focus of the minilesson is to focus narrowly on one particular goal. In a guided reading lesson, although there is a focus goal, there is time to practice, reinforce and assess individuals within the small-group meeting, thus ensuring guided reading success. The lesson format offered here is generic and can be changed to fit the needs of the students, materials, purpose, time, and teaching style. For instance, when teaching an unfamiliar topic from expository text, a text preview should be included. Or, in some instances, the teaching of vocabulary may not be needed prior to reading. Ideal reading lessons contain the following:

Components of a Reading Lesson

Prereading

activate prior knowledge
build background
teach vocabulary (if needed)
predictions

During Reading

purpose setting
mode of reading

Postreading

check predictions
discussion leads: questioning
reader response

Prereading

Activate Prior Knowledge

Begin the reading lesson by activating prior knowledge (Braunger and Lewis 2006) to help the children make connections from what they know to the new (Cooper 2001). Activating prior knowledge increases the likelihood that students will remember and understand what is read while also fostering motivation to read (McEwan 2004). For example, the book *Flossie and the Fox* (McKissack 1986) is the story of a young black girl, Flossie, and the fact that she does not know what a fox is or looks like. Through her partially staged ignorance Flossie manages to trick the fox and get eggs safely to a neighbor. To activate prior knowledge for this book, the teacher can make a semantic web of the word *fox* with the reading group. Most students would have heard of this animal or a similar animal through cartoons and Little Red Riding Hood stories and would be able to add information to a semantic web. As he activates prior knowledge, the teacher is also assessing what the students know about the topic and prepping the students to read. McEwan (2004) refers to activating prior knowledge as priming students' cognitive pumps. It is important that students begin to think about the topic or theme of a story prior to reading, so their minds will be ripe for making connections.

Activating prior knowledge can be done in a variety of ways, and themed ideas will be given in Chapter 5, but some generic activities, which can be done with minimal teacher input, are offered here. Alone or collaboratively, students can

- create a semantic web on a topic

- use a "word splash" and write or discuss what connections the words have for them

- fill in the KW of the KWL or an anticipation guide for expository material

- add their own text to a short paragraph that introduces the topic or theme

- complete a graphic organizer that "sets up a situation" close to the story theme

- create an art project that lends itself to the upcoming theme of the book

- do a hands-on activity that they are familiar with, but lends itself to the topic or theme

Build Background

Building background, the second part of the prereading lesson, occurs when we provide students with more information on the topic prior to reading. In actuality, we are scaffolding the students' learning in that we are preparing them to read successfully. We help students make a bridge from what they know (as assessed in this case on the semantic web) to the new by adding information to help them understand. In essence, Piaget's assimilation and accommodation occurs, not unlike a child learning the difference between a bird and a butterfly, and meaning is enhanced.

Background can be built in a number of ways but needs to be focused on the topic or theme of the material. This sometimes can be very specific information. If students were going to read a book about photosynthesis, then sharing pictures of plants would not be sufficient to build background. Sharing a diagram that shows the process would be perfect; after all, the goal is to make sure the students know the material after reading. Using the diagram for background building will increase their comprehension and aid in their recall. Some generic activities for building background, which can be adapted to the topic or theme and can be done either independently or collaboratively without a lot of teacher guidance, are:

- viewing a marked website with a particular task to do

- previewing a documentary or segment of a video

- reading and analyzing or discussing a chart or diagram

- conducting a short- or long-term research project

- building or creating using clearly written directions

- reading a magazine article or picture book related to the topic or theme

- listening to an "in-house expert" or parent discuss the topic

- studying a map

- examining brochures on the topic or theme

Teach Vocabulary

Most vocabulary is learned through wide reading (Vaughn and Linan-Thompson 2004; Graves 2006) but sometimes vocabulary should be explicitly taught. Working independently with words prior to the reading might be better called "word study." Students can work with words independently or collaboratively in a number of ways. In this lesson format, teaching vocabulary comes prior to reading, but vocabulary can be taught before reading, during reading, and postreading (Cooper 2001).

If the words are new, and what Beck, McKeown and Lucan (2002) call "tier 2," then these words should be explicitly taught through direct instruction by the teacher. Tier 1 words are common, everyday words that need no instruction, such as *glass, table, happy,* and *jump.* Tier 2 words are more sophisticated and enhance a students' vocabulary, yet are not the jargon of content area (tier 3). Tier 2 words are not extremely common but are still conversational words, such as *logical, reluctant*, and *sophisticated*!

In the vocabulary section of the prereading lesson, a teacher has a number of choices in word study. This is not the place to have students work with brand-new tier 2 words. If you have time to explicitly teach the words prior to the students' independent work time, then this would be a perfect opportunity for reinforcement. Giving your students unknown words to work with independently does not set them up for success and may cause confusion of word meaning. Children should have had some degree of exposure to any word study topic. The goal of independent word study activities should be to reinforce meanings or skills. A sampling of purposes for the word study could be: to reinforce tier 2 or tier 3, previously taught words; reinforce word recognition on tier 1 words; work with root words, affixes, tenses, compound words, contractions, number words, color words, or calendar words. Some generic activities for word study that can be done independently or collaboratively are:

- matching game of any sort

- graphic organizer

- word sort

- word bank activities

- "my words" book or dictionary

- magnetic or plastic letters

- crossword puzzle (please, no word searches)

- making vocabulary cards, including a visual

Predictions

Predictions are excellent motivators for reading. They also help teachers assess whether or not a student is using inferential techniques, as good predictions are based on accurate inferences. Students need to be given the guidance to predict and then can do this easily on their own. To guide the prediction tell students to look at the cover of the book, think about what happened in the previous readings, or read just one page of the new reading and write down or draw what they think might happen. This can be done independently or collaboratively without much teacher guidance, by having students:

- use a simple two-space, "T" prediction chart for drawing or writing "What I think will happen" in prereading and "What happened" in postreading (see Appendix 4–1).

- write on a white board or chalk board

- predict in their reading journals

- make a "prediction bag" where they write one or two predictions and put them in a group bag

- fill out an anticipation guide (See sample Appendix 4–2. This is a guide the teacher prepares with stated predictions. The students read and check the statements they think are accurate, or in the case of expository text, what they think is true.)

- complete the KW of a KWL chart for expository text

- use word study computer software activities

During Reading

Purpose Setting

When we set a purpose for reading, we are focusing and motivating the reader. After the students have made their predictions, there is relatively little to do here, but remind them to read to see if their predictions come true. If your purpose is to compare two stories or events, students can review or summarize the first story or event prior to actually reading to keep this purpose in mind.

During Reading

For most guided reading groups, during reading activity is best done with the teacher for the first reading. This way, readers can be guided through the reading section by section, clarifications can be made, and erroneous inferences can be intercepted, and that is the main purpose for guided reading. For more capable groups some reading can be done independently or with a partner. The word *collaboratively* is purposefully not being used here. Once you get more that two students reading together, either one is reading to the rest of the group or round-robin occurs. Neither produces optimal learning. The point of during reading time is to read, and all students must read. Some levels of students do this with complete understanding. They do not have to complete during reading activities because for them this is done unconsciously and stopping to write only spoils the reading. For others, these are great comprehension tools.

Activities that can be done independently or collaboratively during reading with minimal guidance from the teacher include:

- silent reading

- partner reading

- tape-assisted reading

- computer-assisted reading

- comprehension sheets (see example Appendix 4–3)

- sticky note activities (connections, questions, clarifications, I wonders)

Postreading

Check Predictions

Checking predictions aids students in recalling details and facts about the text. This should be done in conjunction with the prereading activity used for making predictions. Although a portion of this can be done independently or collaboratively with minimal teacher guidance, it is important to summarize as a group what really happened. The following activities can be done with minimal teacher guidance.

- Students draw or write what happened on the prediction sheet (see Appendix 4–1).

- Students may discuss what was written on a white board or chalk board.

- Students look at the predictions in their reading journals and write what happened.

- Collaborative groups discuss their "prediction bag" and what really happened.

Discussion Leads: Questioning

Questions are often defined as literal, interpretive, or evaluative. Literal questions have students recall important events, facts, and details in a story. Interpretive questions, called "between the line" questions, allow students to really think about the reading. They learn to infer, to think critically, and to go beyond the literal information in a text. Evaluative questions assume the reader has enough knowledge of the text to make a judgment. The best discussion questions tend to be interpretive questions. A good interpretive question is answered by using facts from the narrative and inferential comprehension to figure out what the author is implying. This lends itself to a deeper and more meaningful discussion. There are two ways that students can answer questions with minimal teacher guidance: write or draw answers to given questions, and discussion groups.

When students write answers to questions, it should not be to quiz them on their understanding. Writing answers can prep students for a dynamic group discussion. When we allow students to write answers to questions, they conscientiously think and organize their thoughts. Students need to discuss these questions, enabling them to learn from each other. Vygotsky (1934, 1978) introduced us to the importance of social learning. When students discuss questions, they learn the interpretation of others, opening their minds to new thoughts and connections.

Reader Response

The area of reader response is the one section of the reading lesson where the teachers' input is minimal, yet instruction remains optimal. The possibilities for reader response seem to be endless, but it is best that the response has a strong connection to the text so student responses show deeper understanding and learning from the text. In the case of narrative, this would be using the literal to support the inferential and evaluative understandings. In the case of expository text, the response would show accurate interpretation of the material read.

Some samples of generic responses from narrative text that need minimal teacher guidance:

- follow-up graphic organizers (such as character or plot analysis)

- journal responses

- poetic responses (such as free verse or couplets)

- posters

- letters

- advertisements

- postcards

- brochures

- sequencing activities

- dioramas

- vocabulary reinforcement activities

Some of the narrative text ideas can also be used for expository text. Ideas more specific to expository include:

- graphic organizers (such as compare/contrast, cause/effect, problem/solution)

- lab reports

- time lines

- PowerPoint slide shows

- chronological order activities

- research reports

- murals

- creating games

Concluding Thoughts

In conclusion, the ideas offered here are basically the tip of the iceberg. Students would do any of these activities during their independent work time. The prereading, during reading, and postreading activities and ideas will be addressed in more depth in the coming chapters. The generic ideas offered are meant to be adapted to your teaching objectives. It is imperative that we continually make sure that the activities chosen meet the goals of the lesson. If a lesson's goal is to have children learn and be able to apply five vocabulary words, a word search does not match this goal. Having the students fold their papers in four sections and have them write the word and the definition and use the word in a sentence and draw a picture or graphic would much better serve this purpose, and has less preparation for the teacher!

Prediction Chart

What I think will happen . . .	What happened . . .

Anticipation Guide

Only Opal, The Diary of a Young Girl by Barbara Cooney (Scholastic, 1994)

Please check all the statements you think will be true in the book.

_____ The girl lives on a farm.

_____ The girl visits a farm.

_____ The girl gets lost in the woods.

_____ The girl moves to a big city.

_____ The girl likes flowers.

_____ The girl milks cows.

_____ The girl does chores.

_____ The girl has lots of friends.

_____ The girl doesn't like to go to school.

_____ The girl gets into trouble.

Comprehension Chart

As you are reading, stop at different times, think about what you read, and do the following:

Write down a prediction.
Draw a scene or fact that you found interesting.
Tell us about something you found confusing.
Ask a question about an event in the book.
Putting just one word in each box, make a two-word description of a character or fact. | | |
Write any words that you had to guess at the meaning.

CHAPTER 5

Prereading Independent Activities

Chapter 4 offered some generic ideas for prereading activities, but in most instances the more tailored an activity is to the text, the better the resulting comprehension. The purpose of this chapter is to share effective prior knowledge and background-building ideas that are specific to particular books, but most activities could be modified to work well with a book or chapter having the same theme.

In a scaffolded reading lesson, prereading activities build the foundation for improving comprehension during reading. Prereading includes activating prior knowledge, building background, and predicting and may also include working with vocabulary. All of these pieces can easily be done well with heavy teacher guidance. Our goal is to incorporate purposeful activities into the prereading portion of our reading lesson that can be done to an exemplary level and that target optimal learning results for our students with minimal teacher guidance.

Prereading activities are used as scaffolding to help prepare students to successfully read a text. We need to tailor these activities to the text being read, keeping in mind that the activity's goal is to enhance comprehension. To get an idea of the importance of prereading, read the following headline and afterward evaluate your understanding of the text as low, medium or high.

"Taunton Pounds Coyle-Cassidy"

After the reading you may decide understanding is low, because you don't have a clue what the headline means except that you assume there are two characters: Taunton and Coyle-Cassidy. Or you might decide your comprehension is medium, as it appears that a wrestler or boxer named Taunton

Figure 5–1. *Semantic Webbing—Activating Prior Knowledge Content Area
Reading*

won over his rival, Coyle-Cassidy. Most likely no one rated their understanding as high, unless they live in the Taunton, Massachusetts area. Had I
done some prereading activities by activating your prior knowledge on football, might you have had more insight as to what the headline is about?
Then had I supplemented that knowledge by building background and
explaining that Taunton High School and Coyle-Cassidy High School,
located in the same city, have been Thanksgiving Day football rivals for
decades and that this annual game took place yesterday—your understanding of the headline would most likely have been high.

We need to do this for our students. It is necessary to give them tools to activate prior knowledge and for us to supplement that knowledge with specific

background information. According to McEwan (2004) activating prior knowledge not only finds out what students know about a topic but also allows us to help students make connections from what they know to their reading. For building background the focus is on unfamiliar material or concepts that the reader will encounter. By building background we send students into a text prepared for success; their interaction with the text has much more depth than if they were reading the words without the knowledge to create complete understanding (Cooper 2001). *Put Reading First, The Research Building Blocks for Teaching Children to Read* (Armbruster, Lehr, and Osborne 2001) a booklet published to guide educators in the five main aspects of reading targeted in the No Child Left Behind program, states that good readers use prior knowledge and experience to aid in comprehension. It does not specifically mention background building. But in essence, helping students build background prior to reading a text means when they actually read the text this background-building information has become prior knowledge.

Ideas on Building Background

Thinking of activities and ideas for building background becomes easier as teachers become more familiar with the various themes books offer. For example, we can discuss activating prior knowledge and building background for the picture book *On Mother's Lap* (Scott 1972). This lovely story is about a young boy, Michael, who is dealing with his jealousy over his newborn sister (a common picture book theme as with *Peter's Chair* [Keats 1964]). The setting of this book appears to be in Alaska as Michael has a reindeer blanket and Eskimo style doll. But the setting is not important in this story and takes a backseat to the theme and Michael's character (as with *Peter's Chair*). Although a teacher could build background about the far north, activating prior knowledge to help students connect with the meaning of the text would suffice. To enhance comprehension for this book the need would be to focus on jealousy over siblings or friends.

Predictions for this book could be done independently in a very active way. Make a copy of the front cover of the book for all the students (the boy is sitting on his mother's lap). Have students draw, label, and paste small pictures of things the boy might want on his mother's lap. After the reading they can check their predictions by circling any item they predicted correctly. As a variation, they can label and draw on sticky notes, and after reading they can remove the wrong predictions. Retell the story by having them draw on sticky notes what did go on the boy's mother's lap and put these items on the picture in the correct sequence.

Arthur's Chicken Pox by Marc Brown (1994) has a reversed theme. The younger sister, D.W., is jealous because her older brother, Arthur, has chicken pox and is getting all the adult attention. There are two specific requirements for background building in this book. We need to make sure students know what chicken pox is and that they have an understanding of circus and circus animals. Most of us would assume that the young students reading this book would know about both chicken pox and the circus. Never assume! Start by activating prior knowledge and assessing what the students know about these topics. Do they know chicken pox is contagious? How long it lasts? It would be best to discuss chicken pox with the students and fill in blank areas before reading.

Although many students may have been to a carnival in their town, they might not know much about the circus. Background building on circuses can be done with minimal teacher help in a variety of ways. A quick check online found three appropriate websites for building background on circus events. One site contained incredible historical poster reproductions, most certainly adding to the background knowledge of this author! These sites can be bookmarked and looked at independently by group members. It would also be possible to share a video of the Barnum and Bailey Circus, which could be watched by the entire group, while you are working with another reading group. Simply put the students in a corner that is visible to your working table. Face the television toward the small group (away from the others), and put the volume on very low. Students will have to stay quiet to hear. You might show a fifteen- or twenty-minute segment, then have students collaboratively write a list of what they saw in the circus.

When More Might Be Best

Some books require a great deal of background building. So much so that teachers must make a professional judgment as to which areas are the most important for text comprehension. With most book topics background building does more than increase comprehension—it also increases student general knowledge and can often extend science or social studies concepts.

In the picture book *The Fourth Question, A Chinese Tale* (Wang 1991), there are a number of areas in which more background would aid in enhancing comprehension. This tale is about a young man, Yee-Lee, who makes a trip to the mountains to ask the wise man why he works so hard and still remains poor. (Okay, so we need this wise man, too.) On his trip, Yee-Lee receives help from others and gathers their questions for the wise man. By the time he arrives at the mountains he has four questions, only one of which is his own. The wise man will only answer an odd number of questions, so Yee-Lee gives him the questions of the others. In the end, Yee-Lee realizes that although he did not get to ask his question, he had found the answer—helping other people had brought him happiness and money.

Thinking over what knowledge students will need for better understanding of this book, the most obvious would be building background on China and the Chinese culture of respect for the elderly and the wise. In addition, students would need to know the definition of a tale, in this instance, a detailed story of an imagined event. The setting is important in this story because the plot is dependent on the cultural and social expectations of the Chinese. The focus of the background building should be around the theme (moral) of the tale: kindness is rewarded. To make connections to this theme while using activities that involve minimal teacher input, you could do one of the following.

- Have students write about a time they have been kind to someone and how they felt afterward.

- Have students interview a partner about a time they have been kind to someone.

- Give partners a scenario to read in which someone needs help. Have them write how they could help this person out. (During the postreading students could add how they would be rewarded for doing this kindness.)

- Have students work collaboratively in groups of three. Each student would explain a time when they had been kind or they could share a kindness they have heard about from others. They could rate this kindness on a "kindness meter," a 1 being weak and a 5 being strong. Evaluating the kindness will give them an avenue for discussion.

- Students could write a list of ways they can be kind to other students in their group, class, or school.

No matter what technique is implemented when fostering students' thoughts about kindness and how it may be rewarded, it is best to share the results of the prereading activity prior to reading. You will be building purpose and helping the students make connections when they begin reading the text.

For predictions with this particular book, a silent picture walk, prior to predicting, is recommended. In a silent picture walk, no one in the group is allowed to talk, including the teacher. This, too, can be done independently. Simply tell the students not to read but just to look at the pictures and use the information from the pictures to write down what they think might happen. Their predictions could then be taped, or if written on sticky notes, placed onto a "mountain" as the group is sharing predictions.

Working with Chapter Books

The format used for activating prior knowledge, building background, and making predictions changes with developmental stage more than the length of the book. In chapter books teachers often activate prior knowledge, build background, and make predictions by chapters or sections of the book, but the procedures can be the same. As an example, *Number the Stars* (Lowry 1990), a Newbery Award winner, is usually read in grades 4 or 5. There are many topics in this book that our students may need to have background on prior to reading. To gain full understanding of the undercurrents of this book, students will need background on World War II, Denmark's role in the war, the resistance movement, Jewish traditions and symbols, Copenhagen's location in respect to Sweden, and the Danish love and admiration for their king. In reality, almost every one of these topics could become a unit. This book, like most, also has a number of smaller topics that could be expanded prior to reading, such as the Danish customs for funerals and details concerning the ways in which Jews were smuggled out of Denmark during World War II.

What needs to be learned prior to reading is the teacher's decision, which is based on prior knowledge assessment. To activate prior knowledge for *Number the Stars*, teachers often use a KWL, which is not the best methodology for this narrative text. The purpose of a KWL is to see what students know about a topic and what they wonder or want to learn. Then students are to read the text and write or summarize together what they learned during the postreading. If a KWL is used on the topic World War II, the students will not get many of their questions answered in *Number the Stars*. The setting, World War II in Denmark, is extremely important to the whole plot of this book but although this book alludes to factual information, it does not offer specific information on the war. Therefore, most likely, the "wonder" or "what I want to learn" portion of the KWL will not be answered. On the "what I learned" portion students will basically summarize facts from the story, which is not the intent of this instructional activity. When reading narrative texts like this, in which the setting and its psychological aspects are crucial to the plot, the recommendation is to simply hold a discussion; for more independent work have partners or groups do a semantic web or a quick write. This helps us to evaluate students' knowledge and rapidly ascertain what background information is needed in order for students to gain full meaning from the text.

Predictions from *Number the Stars* could be done independently by having students write predictions on five-pointed stars. Although it would be important at some point in the book to make sure students understand the significance of the Star of David, the shape of the Star of David is not recommended for the prediction stars. (The Star of David is a symbol of the Jewish religion, much like the cross is to Christians, and should be treated with respect.) On the opposite side of the paper star have students write the support for their predictions. These stars can then be taped to a dark blue board; the group, prior to reading, would discuss the predictions and their support and refer back to the predictions during the postreading time.

Ideas for Book Themes

Books often have the same central theme, and independent activities for activating prior knowledge and building background can be used with books having the same theme. Activating prior knowledge for topics on any expository book can be done by using a KWL, a quick write, an anticipation guide, or a semantic web; by generating questions or answering teacher determined questions; or by a think, pair, share activity (timed, of course!). Any of these ideas can be done independently or collaboratively and all get students thinking about their knowledge on a topic.

Building background on expository texts can be done independently from the teacher by reviewing websites, watching a video or DVD, reading an easier independent read (picture books, brochures, magazine articles), or a four-square miniresearch.. The four-square miniresearch is meant to be a short 20- to 30-minute fact-finding mission. It is not a research project, per se. The purpose is to have students gather some background knowledge on their own, not to make them miniexperts! The teacher needs to gather a variety of material on the expository topic and have it available for the group of students who will be reading the book on that topic. Students will fill in the four-square miniresearch form (see Appendix 5–1) with the information requested, building their own knowledge on the topic as they read and write. As with any new material, the four-square miniresearch should be modeled prior to being done.

As discussed previously, activating prior knowledge and building background for narrative texts is best based on the theme or pertinent information from the book. The chart in Figure 5–2 offers some basic themes found

Figure 5–2. *Ideas for Activating Prior Knowledge and Building Background*

Theme of Book	Ideas for Activating Prior Knowledge	Ideas for Building Background
Someone loses their best friend	Students write a journal entry about a time when they have lost something important.	After placing students with partners have them read three poems about friendship and discuss with each other what friends mean to them.
Dealing with siblings	Have students, in groups of three, tell about a time when they had a great time or a bad time because of a brother, sister, or cousin.	Students watch a five- to ten-minute segment of a sitcom in which siblings are interacting. Then write who the characters are, tell who is younger or older, and explain how they acted. Then tell how they felt about it.
Survival	Have student fill out the survival think sheet (Appendix 5–2).	Read a magazine or online article about surviving in the wilderness, during a hurricane, etc. Make a chart of the most important information.
Family time together	Students brainstorm graffiti style or semantic web things they do with their family (can be done solo or in partners).	Give the students family magazines. Have them cut out pictures of different family units and the activity they are sharing. Put these on a poster board with a written explanation.
Orphaned, looking for a family, homeless	Ask students to connect to the theme (orphaned or homeless). Answer these three questions: What do you think it feels like? What might you do to improve the situation? What can we do now for others in this situation?	Students look at bookmarked websites on orphans. (There are orphaned dog websites, too.) Have students write down their impressions from viewing these sites.
Growing up	Have older students write about things they can do independently from their parents that they could not do when they were younger. Have younger students draw a timeline predicting what they will be doing when they are older. (Start at age five, then seven, nine, eleven, and end at thirteen—that's grown up to them!)	Collaboratively have older students generate a list of challenges they will face growing up (getting a job, a license, going to college, etc.) Give younger students three pictures of a "grown-up" activity. Have them write a sentence about what the grown-up is doing and explain if they can do this now. For instance, a man is cooking and they may help their mother or father in the kitchen.

in picture and chapter books with ideas that need minimal teacher guidance. Most of the activities can be adapted for various levels. Teachers would be supplying the materials in some of the ideas (such as the three poems on friendship).

Figure 5–2. *continued*

Theme of Book	Ideas for Activating Prior Knowledge	Ideas for Building Background
Friends	Older students can write an acrostic poem on "Friendship," having each letter begin the spelling of a trait they would like to find in their friends. For younger children, have them write or draw five things they do with their friends.	In collaborative groups give older students copies of books they would have previously read. Have them chart friendships from each book and write one interesting fact or special event of that friendship. Younger students can listen to a book on tape containing the interactions of friends, such as a Frog and Toad book. They should write and draw a summary of what these friends did together.
Being different (which may be the same as the theme "being accepted")	Give students paper to design a name tag. After they are done, have partners discuss how their name tags came out "different." Have them write down one special detail about each name tag.	Give older students a downloaded biography on Henri de Toulouse-Lautrec and have them make a list of how he was different and what made him accepted. Younger students can analyze pictures of two different breeds of dogs. Have them write the differences and tell what their favorite thing is about each dog.
Being responsible	Give partners scenarios at their age level in which someone must act responsibly. Have them discuss and write down what could be done. For example, for grade 1, there could be milk spilled on the table and floor. What would a responsible person do? In grade 6, someone may find a stray dog. What would a responsible person do?	Have students, in partners, interview school personnel. They can interview the principal, assistant principal, custodian, secretary, etc. Young children can write down two or three things the person is responsible for; older children can go into much more detail.

How Does This Look?

The charts in Figures 5–3 and 5–4 show what might be going on in a classroom with specific books. We assume that the teacher is working with one group while the other two groups are working independently on prereading, during reading, or postreading activities. The following charts show what students are doing for prereading. In these cases, the prereading activity needs minimal teacher guidance. This will not always be true. Some days the teacher may choose to use the reading group time for prereading instruction and give students follow-up for independent work.

Figure 5–3. *Primary Scenario: The teacher has chosen "families" as a theme for her three reading groups.*

Book	Short Summary	Activating Prior Knowledge	Building Background
Night Shift Daddy by Eileen Spinelli	A book written in rhyme about a father and daughter. The father works the night shift, and they put each other to bed.	Have students draw a picture of jobs that their mother, father, or stepfather has. Have them write a short description.	Give students pictures of different jobs. With partners have them discuss what the person is doing. Have them choose one job they might like to do and explain why.
Families Are Different by Nina Pellegrini	This book focuses on a young adopted Korean girl who feels different in her family. The story shows the makeup of different families and explains how they are glued together with love.	Have students draw a picture of their family and label the members.	With partners have students share their family "portraits" and discuss how their families are alike and different.
A Chair for My Mother by Vera B. Williams	This is the story of a young girl, her mother, and her grandmother. A fire destroyed their apartment, and as family they are saving for a nice comfortable chair for mother.	Have children write a list of important things they would lose if a fire were to destroy their home (with no people or animals inside).	Give children furniture ads from the paper. Have students select a chair for their mother, grandmother, or aunt and write why this chair is best for that relative.*

*The pictures of the chairs and the final drafts could be put on background paper and would make a nice group book or bulletin board display.

Book	Short Summary of Focus Chapter	Activating Prior Knowledge	Building Back-ground
Yellow Bird and Me by Jane Hansen	Chapter 3—Plans. The main character, Doris (eleven), has to get a Saturday job to save money to go see her friend Amir, who has moved. Her parents are against this.	Partners will generate a list of ways they can make money.	In groups of four, students will look at the generated list of how to make money. They will discuss each "job" and whether they think they would be allowed to do it.
Sounder by William H. Armstrong	Chapter 2—A poor black sharecropper steals a ham to feed his family. He is arrested and the family dog is shot. The oldest son is concerned about his father and the dog he cannot find.	Have partners brainstorm what they know about Sounder's "family," the boy, younger children, mother, and father.	Have individual students read selected expository material on the life of poor black sharecroppers. They should be prepared to share what they have learned in their reading groups.
Someone Was Watching by David Patneaude	Chapter 10—This is a book about a missing younger sister whom everyone assumed has drowned. Her brother Chris tries to convince his parents in this chapter that she has been kidnapped by someone they know.	Have students write in their journals about a time they knew they were right but no one would believe them. If this has not happened, they can write about a time they tried to convince someone to do something.	Ahead of time, make up a "clue game" where students read one note that gives them a clue to where the next note is hidden. Have about six or seven clues, then let them find a small reward. This ties in with the "clues" Chris notices.

Four-Square Miniresearch

Explain the topic and write at least three facts about the topic.	What did you discover that really interested you in the topic?
Words that are about your topic and what you *think* the words mean.	What connections do you have with this topic? Does it make you think of something you have done, or read before, a movie, television program?

©2007 by Nancy L. Witherell from *The Guided Reading Classroom*. Portsmouth, NH: Heinemann.

Survival Think Sheet

Food	Clothing
Shelter	Warmth

During Reading Independent and Collaborative Activities to Improve Comprehension

As we know, the purpose of guided reading is to guide students through the reading. During this time the teacher explicitly instructs students on reading skills and strategies, clarifies, and encourages questions. Therefore for the majority of the students, and most certainly with very young children and struggling students, it is important to have the first reading of a text done in the guided reading group. Intermediate-level students, depending on their proficiency, will need less guidance and can read more text independently. Reading a text with the teacher first, then applying the strategies in the second or third reading scaffolds students needing more support. Our goal is to have every child become an independent, strategic reader and using guided reading along with independent reading is a good mix for success.

This chapter will offer strategies and activities to scaffold students as they read silently or with partners while the teacher is working with another guided reading group. To scaffold students teachers will need to model independent strategies that students may do while reading. For instance, students could be concentrating on "fix-up" or comprehension strategies as they read, which have been modeled previously by the teacher. Because student reading is being done without the teacher, it is even more important that the text is discussed and shared during the guided reading time. Students, to guide them through their reading, can use the following strategies and activities independently.

Visualizing

Visualization is a technique used in reading to help students comprehend the text. We ask that they make pictures or movies in their minds. This allows the reader to think about the text and apply their reading to the image. Visualization also implies that readers are inferring (Harvey and Goudvis 2000). The reader must think about what the author has said and infer how the scene may look. Visualizing makes reading come alive (Fountas and Pinnell 2001), and the reader feels like he knows the characters as he "sees" them in the story setting. In that way visualizing personalizes reading (Harvey and Goudvis 2000), and when a student visualizes he makes his own image of who and what are in the text. The visual imagery aids the reader in constructing meaning by providing a vehicle to organize thoughts and details and to infer.

Not all children automatically visualize; therefore this comprehension strategy should be modeled. Picture books certainly show students how a text can have a visual image, but some students rely too heavily on the pictures, causing a comprehension problem when the pictures are not there or the pictures depict something other than the written text. In these cases, visualization techniques are an important aid to understanding. To model visualization, the teacher may choose to use a picture book but should not show the pictures. *Froggy Gets Dressed* (London 1992) is a delightful tale about a young frog, who wants to play in the snow, and his mother, who wants him sleeping all winter. He goes out to play, but comes back in several times when his mother reminds him he forgot to put something on (his pants, his shirt, and finally his underwear). Each time he gets dressed he repeats putting on or taking off his mittens, hat, scarf, and boots. Children are very familiar with articles of clothing and can easily make a mental picture of a frog getting dressed, over and over again. Prior to reading, the teacher needs to explain to the students that they are to make "a movie in their head" as the story is read. As the teacher begins to read, she shares her own image of what she sees. The teacher then continues on with the reading, stopping at passages that evoke a strong mental image. Students then share what they visualize with the class or with a partner. Eventually with this book, the illustrator's pictures can be shown. The illustrator, Frank Remkiewicz, has drawn the "movie" that was in his mind.

When the teacher is sure all students understand the process of visualization, this can be done independently when reading or rereading the text. In the primary grades, the choice of book is extremely important. Because we want the children to visualize during reading, they must either be given a passage without pictures or a book in which they can add their own mental images. Although *The Snowy Day* (Keats 1962) has pictures, they are very plain images. This book could be used as long as you tell the students they are to make their own images in their head. Sometimes the text implies a variety of images and the author has only picked one as in *The Adventures of Taxi Dog* (Barracca and Barracca 1990); the readers can visualize the story as they would see it. Books such as *Ira Sleeps Over* (Waber 1972) and *The Perfect Pet* (Palatini 2003) have so many images the illustrators could not put them all into the book, which allows students to make mental images not influenced by the pictures in the text. Once students are reading at a grade 2 or above level, there are numerous chapter books that contain minimal pictures, leaving the readers free to visualize.

Making, Changing, and Supporting Predictions

Strategic thinkers predict. Whether they are analyzing a problem, watching a movie, or reading a book, strategic thinkers are using clues to guess what will or should happen next. Think about watching a movie with friends. How many times does someone say, "I hope this happens." Or "I don't want her to end up with *him!*" These comments are predictions based on inferences gleaned from the movie. The viewer has picked up cues to make her think that something just might happen, or in the second case, that the woman in the film is attracted to an undesirable male. Someone might ask why the predictor thought the woman would even like the guy. Support may be noticed in comments like: "She looked like she was interested"; "She leaned over a certain way," or something in this nature. The next scene may imply something different and new predictions emerge.

The process of predicting during reading is not much different, although it is more of a solo act. When we are reading an exciting book, our unconscious predictions motivate us to get back to the book as soon as we can. Not only do we want to know what is going to happen, but we want to know if what we think is going to happen comes true, which it often does because we have learned the strategy of picking up the cues to hypothesize. Some children do this naturally; others need help in being able to use this strategy successfully. They may need to be explicitly taught how to pick up cues, first from pictures and then from text. They have to be aware that their predictions can be wrong (Jennings, Caldwell, and Lerner 2006) and that the fun of predicting is finding out whether or not the guess was right.

To predict independently during reading, the teacher needs to give thorough directions so students understand exactly what is expected of them. Some students may succeed if the teacher hands them sticky notes and tells the students to stop and predict three times, writing their predictions on the sticky notes. Others need more direction. The teacher should give out three sticky notes and ask students to stick them on three specific pages. The teacher should explain that when the students get to that page they are to write down a prediction before reading the next page.

For very young children, a paper folded in half will be sufficient. First, have the students use the paper as a bookmark on the page that contains a good prediction point. Have the students stop at that page during their reading to draw a prediction and write one sentence about what they think will happen next. After reading, they can use the other half of the paper to draw and write about what actually happened.

In order to aid students in making more accurate predictions, students need to be shown that authors give clues about what might happen and that from these clues they can infer. This can be shown explicitly with just one sentence. For instance, in *Joey Pigza Loses Control* (Gantos 2000), Joey, the main character, has a dog name Pablo and Joey and Pablo are in the car when the author writes, "'Well, Pablo's stomach is about to flip,' I said, warning her" (page 5). In a discussion with children we need to ask, "What is the author hinting at that might happen? Why is the word *warning* in the sentence? What happens when a stomach flips?" These guiding questions will bring students to an accurate prediction. With more practice predictions improve and eventually students are able to predict accurately when working independently. Once students can predict accurately, we challenge them to do more.

Our goal is to enable children to predict, support their prediction, and change predictions when they encounter information that proves their first prediction inaccurate. To accomplish this goal, we take small steps. Once children are making accurate predictions, we know consciously or subconsciously they are taking hints from the texts and inferring correctly. They have support for their predictions. We need to guide them into understanding that sometimes a hint will come that their prediction is not correct, and that they can change their prediction. Children can do this independently during their reading by using a chart (see Appendix 6–1). Students write down what they predict. They are then told to stop at specific pages and decide if they want to change their prediction. They then have to give a reason (support) for changing the prediction or leaving it as is.

I Wonder Statements

I Wonder statements were born to be done independently. When completing I Wonder statements students interact with the text as they make their own meaning and create their own questions. Proficient readers generate questions before, during and after the reading (Keene and Zimmermann 1997). Students catch on to the I Wonder strategy more easily than making and supporting predictions. I Wonder statements can, but do not necessarily, relate to making inferences.

Prior to having students try this independently the teacher needs to model with the students for a higher quality of I Wonder statements. For instance, the book *Over the Wall* (Ritter 2000) begins with the following three sentences: "People say time heals all wounds. I used to think so. Now I know better." The sentences beg for I Wonder statements such as "I wonder what happened that he is hurt?" "I wonder if what happened was serious or something stupid?" "I wonder why he used to think time healed all wounds before, was he happier?" "I wonder why he now knows better?" "I wonder if time does heal all wounds?" The first four questions are all based on inference. The author hints at something horrible having happened and about a better time. The final question simply asks about something the character is denying. All of these questions show interaction with the text. I Wonder statements make asking questions about the reading easier by giving the students a frame to format the question. These statements force students to really think about what is going on in the text and to take an active stance in their reading.

I Wonder statements can be done during reading on sticky notes or on an I Wonder chart (Appendix 6–2). The teacher can tell the students where to stop and write an I Wonder statement. If the preference is not to designate pages, the students can be told to write three to four I Wonder statements as they read. During the postreading discussion, they can explain what they wondered and what made them decide that this place in the text was a good spot to stop and question.

Graphic Organizers

A graphic organizer is created to help students organize, remember, relate to, and comprehend text. This type of organizer should not be used the first time the students are reading the material, especially if the text is narrative. This suggestion is made for two reasons. First, we don't want to make reading something students do not want to do because they equate it with paperwork. Second, we want to be certain that the students actually need the graphic organizer. If the students gain the required comprehension with reading and discussion, there is no need. On the other hand, if students are confused, unable to recall, out of sequence, or struggling with inferences or show a general lack in comprehension, a graphic organizer may offer the support needed.

In some instances a generic organizer may work. A quick search on-line for graphic organizers results in numerous graphic organizers in different styles for a variety of purposes: story maps; beginning, middle, and end charts; problem/solution; cause and effect; T-charts; and Venn diagrams, to name a few. When using a generic graphic organizer, the teacher must choose carefully. For instance, if students in a reading group have difficulty recalling story elements and retelling, story mapping would assist them in this skill (characters, setting, problem, attempts to solve, and solution). Some generic story maps place a specific number of attempts to solve and leave blank spaces for three to five events. If the story the students are mapping has only two attempts to solve, seeing three to five blank spaces for these two attempts would confuse some children. So, the solution is to make a graphic organizer or find a generic form that has one big box for the attempts to solve so the numbers will not inhibit learning.

On the other hand, a generic T-chart graphic organizer can be used easily for a number of purposes. If students need help to remember details, such as characters' actions, one side of the T-chart can be labeled "Characters," the other side "Action." As children reread, they can fill in the chart. When the guided reading group meets, students will be prepared with details to help them in the discussion. Once students are successful with the T-chart being used for this purpose, the teacher can make the task more difficult by adding a column and making a three-chart. The third column might be labeled "Results of the action." When using this three-chart, the students must also supply how the characters' actions affected the plot. T-charts can be used for a number of other purposes simply by guiding the students with the two top labels. (See Figure 6-1.)

Figure 6–1. *Uses for T-Charts*

Instructional Purpose	Label Side One	Label Side Two
Determining importance	Important	Interesting
Relating text	Events	Connections
Forming evaluative statements	Events or actions	My opinion
Clarifying	The event or action	My question or what I don't get
Word study through context	The vocabulary word	What I think it means

Think Abouts

Students can use Think Abouts to share their thought processes as they construct meaning from the text (Witherell and McMackin, 2002). Think Abouts should be modeled by using think alouds. In the strategy of think alouds the teacher reads through the text and shares his thinking out loud. For instance, Mr. Kennedy is reading from the book *Shiloh* (Naylor 2000) and makes comments about the dog that he had as a child. When Marty hides Shiloh against his parents' wishes, Mr. Kennedy voices his thoughts that he would have kept Shiloh hidden, too, because no dog deserves to get beat up by anyone, not even the owner. In essence, Mr. Kennedy is exposing to the students the meandering of his thoughts as he interacts with the text and constructs his own meaning.

When following the gradual release of responsibility model, Mr. Kennedy at some point stops sharing his thinking and starts asking his students to share theirs. When they are successful at sharing their thoughts they are ready for Think Abouts, which can easily be done independently with a T-chart or sticky notes. In the first column of the T-chart students should be told to write down the action or event, and in the second column what they thought about while reading. These thoughts should be shared as part of the discussion during the group's guided reading session or independent group discussion.

Making Connections

How many times have we stopped children from going "off tangent" in the classroom? The teacher reads a story about chicken pox and gets inundated with comments from students—when they had chicken pox, almost had chicken pox, their little cousin had chicken pox, and, oh yeah, Uncle Pete did too. We know we have to rein in these comments, but we also know that making connections with text helps readers to construct their own meaning. According to Keene and Zimmermann (1997) there are three types of connections that readers make: text-to-self, text-to-text, and text-to-world. It is through these connections that readers create meaning. Text-to-self connections indicate that the students have read something in the book that reminds them of something in their own life. Text-to-text connections occur when the readers relate information in the current text to a previously read one. Finally, text-to-world connections are a result of the reader making a connection with something or someone else.

Connections can be done independently, much like Think Abouts. The teacher can have the students use sticky notes placed at the appropriate place in the book or a T-chart labeled with "What the text said" and "My connection." As students become more sophisticated at making and recognizing connections, the teacher can stretch the learning by using a three-chart and adding a column that has students identify the type of connection (text-to-self, text-to-text, text-to-world).

Discussion Groups or Circles

Literature circles are used to promote conversations about reading and are usually used in the postreading section of a reading lesson. The purpose of during reading discussion groups is to give readers, who may not do their best independently, support while they read. For management purposes, it might be best to keep the discussion group down to three or four. If you have a group of six reading *Maniac Magee* (Spinelli 1990), it would be advantageous to divide the reading group into subgroups of three to do the independent reading. The mode of reading would be silent. The students read silently and stop at designated places (one or two pages or a short chapter) and discuss what they are thinking. In following the reciprocal teaching method, one student could begin with summarizing the short section. Otherwise, students can simply share comments, connections, questions, and clarifications to aid in their construction of meaning.

During reading discussion groups may initially be difficult to manage. Teachers must make sure students understand the usefulness and seriousness of book discussions and that students understand their independent group discussion can follow the pattern of the discussions during their reading group time. Begin by modeling with the fishbowl technique. The teacher works with a small group of students while the rest of the class observes what the group is doing. Group procedures and expectations should be modeled during this time. The fishbowl group should silently read the text to the designated spot and let conversation flow naturally. If students seem to be stymied, the teacher can make a connection comment to help the conversation flow. After the fishbowl modeling, the teacher should debrief with the group and the class. This discussion should include a review of what was seen, what worked during the discussion, and a summarization of expected behaviors.

Partner Reading

Students often partner read when teachers are working with other groups. Nettles (2006) suggests six ways students can read together as partners:

- back and forth, in which students take turns reading

- character roles, in which students decide which character they will read, and share the rest of the page (although it goes smoother if they choose the character and alternate reading the rest of the page)

- keeping track, in which one student keeps track with her finger as the other reads (could use ruler, too)

- whisper together, in which the students read chorally

- say something, in which partners read silently and stop at designated points to discuss their reading

- question the author, in which partners read silently and stop at a designated point and make up a question to ask the author

Following are some additional ideas to scaffold and vary partner reading.

- Think Abouts—Partners stop where designated and share what the reading makes them think about.

- Fluency focus—Partners take turns reading, then reread their favorite part.

- Repeated reading for fluency—Partners take turns reading, then when done they switch with another set of partners and read again (the two partners teams must be set up ahead of time).

- Summarizing—Partners take turns reading pages, and the listener summarizes what was read before reading on.

- Visualization—Have partners stop and describe to each other what they visualize at designated pages in the reading.

Tape-Assisted Reading

Some students need a great deal of scaffolding to read independently. It is sometimes advantageous to allow students to listen to a tape of the book as they read. Tape-assisted reading can be set up to the needs of your students. For example, it may be that the teacher wants students who need tape-assisted reading to do Think Abouts. Students can be told on what pages to stop the tape so that they can write down their connections or what they are thinking about.

There are advantages to teacher-produced tapes. They can be read slowly enough that students can easily follow. The teacher can direct students on tape. For instance, after a certain part of the text has been read, the teacher can direct the student to stop the tape and predict or connect.

Vocabulary Strategies

When we discuss students being strategic, the ability to acquire word knowledge is paramount. It is well known that most vocabulary words are learned through wide reading (Armbruster, Lehr, and Osborne 2001). We need to teach children how to be independent word learners. If the word meaning cannot be deciphered from clues in the text and if the word is important to the meaning of the text, then it should be explicitly taught in prereading. On the other hand, the discovery of word meaning is an extremely important part of reading. There must be explicit instruction on the strategies of learning new words while reading (look at context, look back, reread, read ahead, look at pictures, look for a word within the word, look for familiar affixes).

One strategy for younger children is BEST (Witherell 1995). As an independent strategy, students are taught to look at the *B*eginning of the word, the *E*nd of the word, the whole *S*entence, and finally anywhere else in the *T*ext (pictures, surrounding sentences, captions). Once students have mastered this strategy, teachers can remind students to do their BEST. An independent strategy for older students is SSCD (Devine 1987). Students are taught to use *S*ound clues, *S*tructure clues, *C*ontext clues and if necessary the *D*ictionary.

When having students work with vocabulary during reading, independent strategies should be employed. One way of assessing students in their use of these strategies is to have children write word meanings or what they think the word means as they read the word in context. It is highly recommended that this be done during a rereading, so as not to interrupt students' construction of meaning as they read the text. Picture yourself in the middle of a murder mystery, reading the sentence, "The man eyed Edna as she surreptitiously slid the fireplace poker behind the couch." Would you want to stop and look up *surreptitiously?*

Figure 6–2. *Primary-Level During Reading Activities*

Primary Level	Book and Summary	During Reading Activity
Low level	*Brown Bear, Brown Bear, What Do You See?* (Martin 1983) Brown Bear, what do you see? leads to a different animal on each page.	Have students partner read. To scaffold, one student can look ahead, if they both can't read the type of animal, as the following page has a picture of the animal. This aids students to read independently.
Middle level	*Mouse Paint* (Walsh 1989). Mice get into primary color paint and end up all colors.	Give students strips of paper (bookmarks) that are red, yellow, blue, orange, green, and purple. Have students place the bookmarks with the correct color in the book.
High level	*In the Piney Woods* (Schotter 2003). In this intergenerational story a young girl loses her beloved grandfather around the same time her new nephew is born.	This book is meant for discussion. A discussion group should stop at each page and share their thoughts about the reading.

Figure 6–3. *Intermediate-Level During Reading Activities*

Intermediate Level	Book and Summary	During Reading Activity
Low level	*The Patchwork Quilt* (Flournoy 1985). An intergenerational tale about a quilt of family cloth put together by three generations.	Give students three to four different-colored sticky notes and have them do Think Abouts as they read. When discussing these in the guided reading group, put them together in quilt-like fashion.
Middle level	*My Daddy Was a Soldier* (Ray 1990). This book describes life in the United States during WWII while a father went off to war.	This book will need to be broken down in sections, as it is too long to be read at one time. I Wonder statements would work very well with this book.
High level	*Josie's Troubles* (Naylor 1992). This hilarious chapter book is about two girls and their plant- and pet-sitting business.	The reading of this book will need to be broken into chapters. This is a great book for connections done independently to be discussed in the guided reading group.

Book Ideas

The charts in Figures 6–2 and 6–3 give ideas that can be applied with particular books for independent during reading activities. Figure 6–2 suggests primary-level activities and Figure 6–3 suggests intermediate-level activities.) If students are doing reading as an independent activity, they must be held accountable for this reading during their guided reading time. This can be done by having them share the results of their independent time by discussing the text and asking interpretive questions to assess the depth of students' comprehension.

Predictions

What I Predict	Changing My Prediction	My Reasons to Change or Not!

©2007 by Nancy L. Witherell from *The Guided Reading Classroom*. Portsmouth, NH: Heinemann.

I Wonder Chart

Stop reading on page _____.

? I wonder _____

_____

• •

Stop reading on page _____.

? I wonder _____

_____

• •

Stop reading on page _____.

? I wonder _____

_____

• •

Stop reading on page _____.

? I wonder _____

_____

• •

Stop reading on page _____.

? I wonder _____

_____

7

Postreading Independent and Collaborative Activities as Follow-up

There was a time when postreading follow-up was workbooks and ditto sheets, rarely connected to the actual stories in the basal text. Usually there was a skills sheet and application of the vocabulary, but no more thought about the actual reading. This chapter is making a case for both, the application and reinforcement of skills and strategies, and deeper, more intense thoughts about the reading. Often postreading time may involve rereading, so students will be able to respond to the reading with accurate and thorough knowledge of the text information. In the previous chapters it was recommended that certain strategies were best done during a rereading. This would occur during the students' independent work time.

When planning postreading responses for guided reading groups, it is sometimes hard to measure the amount of time students will need to complete the assigned tasks. Try to estimate time as closely as possible, but better to err on the side of having time left over. Students should always have books available for independent reading time. When students have completed their reading response, they should automatically go into their independent reading books. What's the worst that can happen? They get an extra ten minutes to read? (For those of you who are skeptical about that last question, ideas for management strategies will be offered in Chapters 13 and 14.)

Postreading responses and activities should always be curriculum oriented, purposeful, and based on effective practices. We know that learners need multiple opportunities to interact with text in purposeful and meaningful ways (Braunger and Lewis 2006). Through reader response techniques teachers facilitate the process of the reader connecting to the text and thereby constructing their own meaning (Farris, Fuhler, and Walther 2004). We want the follow-up responses to the text to focus on meaning, guiding students to extract more understanding. Instruction should help readers make sense of written language (Braunger and Lewis 2006) and we must be mindful that responses to reading should facilitate that construction of meaning.

The ideas given in this chapter will focus on reader response to narrative and informational text with ideas that can be implemented individually or collaboratively. In addition, there is also a section on vocabulary reinforcement. Also, although not expanded upon in this chapter, skill reinforcement may be done at independent time. Ideally, the skill reinforcement would connect to the reading, but it can just as easily connect to a minilesson in which a need had been identified (such as pluralizing) or connected to the district curriculum.

Responding to Fiction/Narrative text

Checking Predictions

Sounds simple enough, checking predictions, but in reality coming to closure with predictions is often overlooked. For example, in a read-aloud, teachers frequently begin with, "What do you think this book is going to be about?" The question appears to have dual purposes, one of predicting and one of activating prior knowledge. Students enthusiastically answer, and the read-aloud begins. At some points in the story, the teacher may pause and ask if students would like to change their predictions. At the end of the reading, predictions are often not even mentioned.

Predictions are more than a motivational tool or the purpose-setting agenda. As mentioned in Chapter 4, predictions are inferences. In postreading students can be held accountable for why their predictions were right or wrong. As they become strategic readers, we want them to sharpen this strategy by verifying what clues allowed them to predict correctly or what actually happened if their prediction was wrong, what misled them to give the wrong prediction.

Children check their predictions individually or collaboratively. Using the T-chart for predictions, the teacher tells the students to label one column "Predictions" for prereading and "What actually happened" for postreading, or on a three-chart add the label, "Clue for prediction." In this way during postreading students may analyze their predictions. Very young children can simply draw in a "post" box what actually happened and write one or two sentences about it. During their reading group, they can share the drawn summaries and orally explain why their predictions were right or wrong.

Sequencing (Write or Draw)

To retell a story accurately students must be able to have the sequence correct. Usually we discuss the sequence of stories as having a beginning, middle, and end as when young children use a paper with three boxes to portray the beginning, middle, and end. They should be encouraged to write about each one also. Older student can use the boxes too, but they should write about the events in the beginning, middle, and end of the story. In Mr. Arturo's fourth-grade class, he gives each student three index cards. He has the students write the beginning, middle, and end on each card. Students then scramble their index cards and exchange with a partner. The partners then read the other student's three index cards and sequence them in order from beginning to end. The partners tell each other whether or not they are correct. Mr. Arturo explains that an incorrect result of the order could be the result of the writer (or artist) not putting enough detail into their writing (drawing) or the reader missing important information from the writing. Students who have incorrectly sequenced cards reread together and discuss the "why." Mr. Arturo pays particular attention to this as he strives to improve students' details in writing and their skill in reading for detail.

For younger children props or stick puppets are great for sequencing skills. If a whole retelling is not needed, sequencing can be done with just part of the story. Using the book pictures of characters and main settings, make small copies for students or allow them to draw their own figures and settings. Glue these onto popsicle sticks or straws to make stick puppets. Have children retell the story or a part of the story to see if anything is omitted.

Story Components

Students can use a variety of graphic organizers to analyze story components as a postreading activity. Story components, or story grammar, include: characters, setting, problem, attempts to solve, and solution. Any web search typing in "graphic organizers" will bring you to numerous story maps. Model and practice story maps prior to assigning as an independent task. Students completing a story map collaboratively should be required to write down more information. Young or struggling students can use pictures to complete the story map. The goal is to see if students can identify the different story map components and if they can recall the facts and events in the story.

Primary grades have a cute project using large-sized construction paper to make a story map. The paper is folded in half lengthwise and slits are

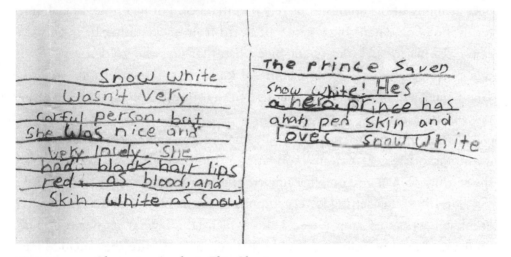

Figure 7–1. *Character Analysis Flip Chart*

made to the halfway mark (for a flip chart type of look). Usually four sections are cut, and the paper is folded so the cut sections are on top. Students draw the main character on one section, and then the setting, problem, and solution, respectively. On the inside half, students write about these components. (See sample of character analysis, grade 2, Figure 7–1.)

Each individual story component can be the focus of a postreading activity, resulting in students gaining a deeper understanding of the plot. For instance, students can use a graphic organizer to analyze the main character or write a character description in their journals. When modeling the writing of a character description both physical and personality traits should be included, as long as the narrative gives facts or inferences on both.

An interesting and worthwhile project with characters, making a relationship tree, fosters students' thinking to go beyond individual character and into story aspects that link character together. Think about reading a historical saga that includes generations of families, and the author very kindly includes a family tree near the front of the book. Readers rely on that family tree to keep their thinking clear about specific characters. Students sometimes need this support in their reading, and they can create a relationship tree of their own. In collaborative groups, students would draw the connections from character to character as they appear in the book. Depending upon the book, this could end up being a long-term project. For instance, in the book *A View from Saturday* (Konigsburg 1996), there are number of characters that relate in a variety of ways, and this would have to be done in almost every chapter. But in a short book like *The Jolly Postman or Other People's Letters* (Ahlberg and Ahlberg 1986), this might be completed in one setting. Be aware that the relationships in this book are very difficult to connect as many of the connections rely on inference. For example, one character in the book, Giant Bigg, gets a postcard from Jack stating he is on vacation with his mother and Giant Bigg's hen that lays the golden eggs. So in one postcard we have Jack whom we know has a relationship with the Giant, Jack's mother, and the Giant's hen that now belongs to Jack—rather complicated.

The setting of a story can be easily analyzed by having students complete a graphic organizer. A more motivating response is to have students draw the setting while mandating specific criteria. For instance, in the book *Holes* (Sachar 1998), the setting is very important to the plot. The main character, Stanley, is sent to Camp Green Lake, which is not what its name implies. Students should be told to draw the setting, making sure they include facts given in the story, and to also suggest the mood of the story through the drawing. A few sentences explaining what is happening in the drawing should be included. A scene from *Holes* might be Stanley, in town, with sneakers on his shoulders; digging holes would be at Camp Green Lake; a scene of the mountains might be the boys' escape. Each of these particular scenes would depict a different mood.

When examining the attempts to solve, and the solution, students employ sequencing and analytical skills. The character and setting are usually very factual. Attempts to solve and sometimes the solution may require inferential comprehension. Furthermore, some complicated plots (the attempts and solution) are very difficult to follow. In the book *Someone Was*

Watching (Patneaude 1993), Chris and his best friend refuse to believe Chris' younger sister has drowned, and they try in a variety of ways to find her kidnappers, if there really are kidnappers. This suspenseful mystery drama uses clues to lead and mislead the reader. Keeping track of the attempts to solve the problem would most likely be a long-term project or a review that could be done in a couple of days. In contrast, in the Caldecott-winning picture book *My Friend Rabbit* (Rohmann 2002), the plot is easily followed. The problem is a toy airplane stuck in a tree; the attempt to solve has Rabbit placing one animal on top of another to reach the airplane. The solution is obvious but gets somewhat complicated with the addition of all the animals needed to reach the toy airplane.

Story Frames

Story frames ask for the same information as story maps using a summary format which assists students in sequencing their writing For example:

In this story _____ is the main character.
_____ wanted to _____. Then
_____. When the story ends
_____.

Sometimes the language used in story frames does not fit the story the students are reading and must be adjusted. The previous example is for one character. If there are two main characters as in a Frog and Toad story, this would be extremely confusing to the students and must be adapted. The teacher could use the example given here and tailor it to the story. Even the verb *wanted to* may not be the best but can be substituted with *tried to* or taken out completely and replaced with _____'s (the main character) problem was _____.

Piggyback Stories

A piggyback story is a story that is written in the same pattern as a story the children read. Teachers often use *Brown Bear, Brown Bear, What Do You See?* (Martin 1983) to have the class produce a story that involves each student in the class and who they see. A number of books make terrific piggyback stories simply because of their text structure. For instance, a book that offers a repetitive line, such as *Have You Seen My Cat?* (Carle 1987), could easily become, Have You Seen My *Anything!*

Any pattern book can be made into a piggyback story, even a fairy tale, which begins with "Once upon a time" and ends with "and they lived happily ever after." Or a circle book, which ends and begins at the same place. Another familiar pattern is a sequence story, such as a story that goes through the days of the week, or the alphabet. A more complicated alphabet pattern book is *Q Is for Duck: An Alphabet Guessing Game* (Elting and Folsom 1980). In this book *Q* is for duck because ducks quack, *R* is for lions because lions roar, and the whole alphabet is given in the same manner. This book could be used as a model of a very challenging piggyback book by having students write the alphabet in this fashion for a content area. For example in weather "*R* is for clouds because of the rain, *S* is for rainbow because the sun comes out," and so forth.

Writing Letters

Letters can be written as a postreading activity for a variety of purposes. In *Sarah, Plain and Tall* (MacLachlan 1985), teachers often have the students write the letters from Caleb or Anna, since they are not seen in the story, and the reader must infer what has been said. *Dear Mr. Henshaw* (Cleary 1981) is often used as a spin-off for students to write to their favorite author. The book mentioned previously, *The Jolly Postman or Other People's Letters* (Ahlberg and Ahlberg 1986), is often used for students to write their "letter/postcard" book. A similar book, *With Love, Little Red Hen* (Flor Ada 2001), contains a series of letters to various storybook characters. Don't be fooled by the name of this book. It is not an easy read and contains some wonderful vocabulary. (This book also has unusual character connections and would be a great source to model the relationship tree.)

Another use for writing letters is to write to characters in a book. When students write their letters, they need to consider the character's personalities, their relationships, and the events in the plot. Letters can be written for various reasons and should stem from the plot of the book. This may be advice on a range of topics: how to solve a problem, how to get better grades, how to make friends, how to make money, how to get along with someone, and even, as in the case of Pippi Longstocking, how to dress. Some other letter writing ideas include the following:

- Whether characters are best friends or worst enemies, students can team up and write letters to each other as two of the characters in the book.

- The students can pretend to be one of the characters and write a letter to Dear Abby. They can then answer each other's Dear Abby letters.

- If there is a good cause featured in the book, students can write a politician and advocate.

- A letter can be written to the author of the book asking questions about the plot.

Writing a Prequel or Sequel

When we fall in love with characters we never want to leave them, and we want to learn as much as we can about them. Students can create their own links to a character's life by writing a prequel, events that happened before a story began, or by writing a sequel, events that happen after the story ended. In the book *Sarah, Plain and Tall* (MacLachlan 1985) we meet Anna, Caleb, and their father Joseph after the death of the children's mother and Joseph's wife. Most readers would love to know how Joseph met his first wife and the story of their lives together—the prequel to the book.

In the Caldecott winner mentioned previously, *My Friend Rabbit* (Rohmann 2002), Rabbit is constantly in trouble and the book ends with Rabbit and his friend Mouse in a toy airplane stuck up in a tree. Rabbit says (again), "Not to worry, Mouse, I've got an idea." That idea would make a wonderful sequel, and if students model the sequel after the way the book is written it would be unique, as a few pages of the story are told in just pictures.

Almost any book read in the classroom can have a prequel or sequel. Books with straight story lines, in which there is no problem or climax, would not be useful for either. Students must understand that when writing a sequel or prequel the characters must stay true to form. A character that is greedy most likely remains greedy, unless, of course, the purpose of the sequel is to "change the character's stripes."

Readers' Response Through Journal Writing and Interpretive Questions

There are so many things that can be written in a reading journal, such as predictions, T-chart with predictions and what actually happened, or a T-chart with summary and opinion. A reading journal's purpose is to respond to the story in some way. The response could be simply a Think About. For instance, a teacher tells students that after reading the chapters they are to write and explain what they are thinking about. Reader response theory allows students to become thoughtful meaning makers and aids them in interpreting the text, and with response students are more likely to deepen their comprehension (Barton and Sawyer 2004).

A journal is a wonderful vehicle to think "beyond the lines" and make connections. A beyond the line question asks students to go beyond the story. In the case of Caleb and Anna in *Sarah, Plain and Tall,* the response question might be "How would you feel if you were going to meet a strange woman who might become your mother?" We want to guide students to write to gain a deeper understanding of the story.

In addition, we want students to read between the lines and interpret what the story is saying. Answering interpretive questions aids in critical thinking and helps students understand what the author means (Manzo, Manzo, and Estes 2000). Although it is recommended that the questions come directly from the plot, there are some generic questions that can be used for a number of books. Some questions leading to thoughtful journal responses follow.

- How would you feel if what happened in the book happened to you?

- Who is your favorite character and why?

- Who is your least favorite character and why?

- What do you think the character should have done?

- Do you think the solution was fair?

- If you could go any place with one of the characters, which one would you choose, where would you go, and why would you go there?

- What would you like to have changed in this book and what would that have resulted in?

- Are we meant to blame the _____ for what he did?

- Tell me about the setting of the story—what did you like or dislike about it?

- If you could change one event in the story, which one would you change and how would you change it?

- Did you read any sections that were confusing? Explain why it seemed confusing.

- How did the setting influence the plot? Could this story have happened elsewhere?

- Pick a quote you liked from the last chapter and explain what it means and why you like it.

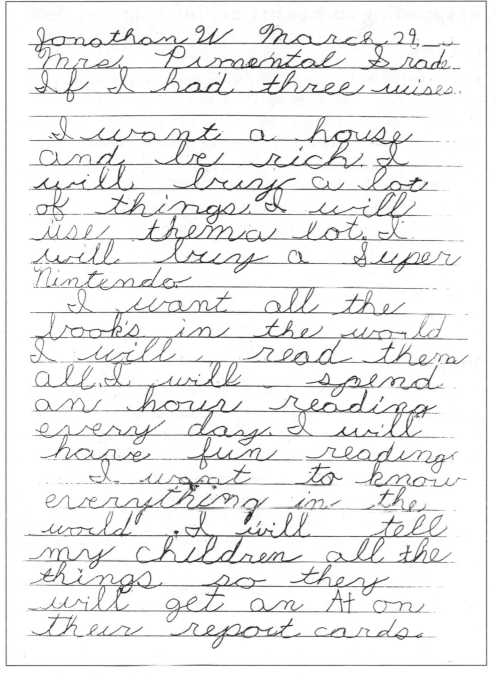

Jonathan W   March 29,__
Mrs. Pimental 3rade
If I had three wishes.

I want a house
and be rich. I
will buy a lot
of things. I will
use them a lot. I
will buy a Super
Nintendo.
I want all the
books in the world
I will read them
all. I will spend
an hour reading
every day. I will
have fun reading.
I want to know
everything in the
world. I will tell
my children all the
things so they
will get an A+ on
their report cards.

Figure 7–2.   *Three Wishes*

■ What else would you like to have known once the story had ended?

In the book *Three Wishes* (Clifton 1976), a young girl finds a lucky penny, which is to give her three wishes. Figure 7–2 shows a third-grade response as Jonathan writes about his own three wishes.

Responding to Nonfiction/Information Text

L of KWL

Kerri, a student teacher, has prepared a wonderful lesson to showcase to her college supervisor. She is reading *The Mouse and the Motorcycle* (Cleary 1965) with one of her reading groups and does a KWL on mice prior to reading. The students know a lot about mice and have wonderful questions, such as "Do mice hibernate like bears?" After the reading, the problem becomes clear—the children, although responding to the Learn column, can't answer their generated questions. And the L column is full of information about the mouse on the motorcycle, but not mice in general. The problem here is that the KWL chart was designed for informational text. Doing a KWL on mice while reading this book will not produce an effective result. If students were reading a nonfiction book on mice, the KWL chart would be perfect.

Summarizing

The strategy of summarizing has been identified as a critical strategy for use in learning from text (Braunger and Lewis 2006). In summarizing, students must capture the major points of a text and add details for support (Caldwell and Leslie 2005). Asking students to independently summarize an informational text during postreading not only increases their understanding but can also be used as an informational assessment resource for the teacher. When groups summarize, it is often difficult to distinguish what each student is contributing. An independent written summary offers assessment data when answering the following: Does the student state the main ideas? Can the student differentiate between what is important and what is superfluous? Does the student use the look back strategy to check information? Does the student use look back to make sure the vocabulary and the spelling are correct? If a teacher finds a number of individuals with an answer of No to these questions, it is time to form a skills group on summarization techniques.

The Four or Five W's

Students can do a quasisummary by answering the four or five W's after reading an informational text, the "who, what, when, where, and why" factors. The four W's come into play because not all informational texts have a "who." If students are reading an article on the conservation of fuel, the what (conservation of fuel) is easily identified, but there may be no who. Students should also glean from the article the when, where, and why factors.

This activity offers support for students who have problems putting in important details when summarizing.

Responding to Questions on Informational Text

For the most part questions on informational text are literal, as we want students to know the facts. But, literal (by the line) questions may not be the best strategy to get students to know the facts and think about the material. It is hard to give generic questions about informational text, but here are some questions that can be easily tailored to different topics.

- What is the purpose of the text you just read?

- What facts did you find the most interesting and why?

- How can you apply the information in this text to your everyday life?

- Explain the cause-and-effect relationship in this text.

- Explain the problem and solution in the text. Would you have considered a different solution? Why or why not?

- Do you agree or disagree with what the author is explaining?

- Compare the information in this text to what you read yesterday.

Using Graphic Organizers with Informational Text

One effective way to have children summarize a chapter is through graphic organizers. Teachers can give out cause-and-effect charts, problem-solution, compare-contrast, or chronological order graphic organizers depending on the text structure. Doing a semantic webbing on the text will help students interact with details from the text. If students are familiar with graphic organizers, they can create their own. Students should be told that the connections must be evident. There is some excellent commercial software that helps students with graphic organizers (and outlining) such as Kidspiration or Inspirations.

Categorizing

Categorizing information makes the student think about the material read. Text should be selected for this purpose. For instance, text on the classification of life from living to nonliving could lead to categorization. Students can decide the categories or teachers can give specific categories.

Sometimes stating selected categories forces students to think in a different way. If students were reading about the endangered species in your state, they might categorize under the labels of fish, amphibians, reptiles, mammals, birds, and plants. When putting the endangered species under these categories they may find one category, which in this case is a type of vertebrate animal, has more endangered animals than another. This may lead to speculation into the cause.

Time Lines

Time lines or products that direct chronological order help students in sequencing information. For some events, such as historical, this can be crucial to comprehending and may aid students in visualizing the cause-and-effect components of a relationship. Time lines can be as simple as the four seasons when applied to the growing of wheat or as complex as when pinpointing events from minute to minute in an explanation of a shuttle launch. Depending on the goal of the teacher's lesson, a time line may be best as a long-term project. Short projects, like the four seasons, can be done during one or two independent work times. On the other hand, one done on the life of Abraham Lincoln may be best done over a longer time period, so students can include the historical events surrounding his election and presidency.

Mnemonic Devices

True confessions: I used mnemonic devices to make it through my comprehensive exams as I acquired my doctorate. Mnemonic devices are sayings or letter associations that create a word or sentences to aid us in remembering. For instance, if someone were to ask the names of the five Great Lakes, the mnemonic device HOMES works every time (Huron, Ontario, Michigan, Erie, and Superior). Mnemonic devices assist students in remembering information (Moore, Moore, Cunningham, and Cunningham 2003). When teaching third grade my use of a made-up mnemonic device, FARM B, helped my students (and me) remember the five classifications of vertebrate animals (fish, amphibians, reptiles, mammals, and birds).

Students are motivated when creating mnemonic devices to remember information about a topic. They enjoy this task and have to think critically about the material to write a mnemonic. They can create mnemonic words or sentences, such as the lines on the music scale, "every good boy does fine." Doing this in groups of two or three works well and leads to a creative solution.

Journal Writing in Response to Informational Text

The focus on journal writing with informational text is different from that of narrative. Journals can be used for a variety of reasons; although it is best to keep these reasons specific to the information read, some generic ideas follow.

■ Students could keep a summary of what was read.

■ To infuse art into learning, the journal could be a graphic and artistic display of what is being read.

■ The 3, 2, 1 entry: students would write three things they learned, two things they had questions about, and one reaction to the reading.

■ Double entry journal: use one side for facts, the other for the reader's reaction.

■ Students could use concept mapping, showing connections to concepts through a graphic organizer.

■ Students could respond to a specific issue brought up in the text.

Possible Sentences

Possible sentences (Buehl 2001) use key concept words from the reading. The teacher gives the students a list of words they may use in sentences. The students are to make up sentences that could *possibly be true* using two of the words. Students who are able to make up possible sentences are showing understanding of the information learned and sometimes applying that information differently. For instance, for a book about planets the teacher may choose all the names of the planets as key concepts words, along with the words *moon*, *asteroids*, and *sun*. Possible sentences are: "Earth and Mars are neighbors" and "Jupiter is the planet after Mars." On the other hand "The Earth and Uranus are neighbors" and "The Earth revolves around the moon" would be incorrect sentences. This technique can also be used prior to reading. Then students would read to check if their sentences could be possible.

Reinforcement of Vocabulary

Word Study

Vocabulary can be taught before, during, and after reading. Postreading is an opportune time to give students activities to reinforce vocabulary and to reinforce strategies used in learning new words. This can be done in their journals or students may have a designated word study book. For emergent readers word study may be a variety of phonics activities and techniques, such as independent phonics games, gameboards, manipulatives, or computer phonics/word games.

Primary-Level Ideas

Reinforcement of Phonics

There are a multitude of inexpensive phonics games on the market. These games should be first played in a skills group, and the independent time should be used for reinforcement. Leveled reading groups and skill groups do not necessarily contain the same students, and differentiation should occur. One student may be working with manipulatives matching onset and rimes; another two students may be using manipulatives working with the VCe rule (Vowel, Consonant, silent e); yet another student could be working on manipulatives reinforcing affixes. This differentiation is not as difficult as it seems. One of the advantages of working with small groups in guided reading lessons is that teachers get to know each student as a learner. They see the "fumbles" and use annotated notes to remember what students' needs are.

Word Recognition

Students need reinforcement of words; they need constant repetition to reinforce their learning. Although there are games and manipulatives on the market, word recognition truly has to come from the words students are reading in their text. To build fluency we want students to use these words over and over again in different ways that not only reinforce word recognition but also word meaning (Prescott-Griffin and Witherell 2004).

Following are a few activities that will reinforce word recognition.

- Sentence match: Have cutout words that match the sentences in the book. Have students make the same sentence as in the book by putting the words in correct order. Have them read the sentence to a partner.

- Word sorts: Closed or guided word sorts (Cunningham 2005) give students the words they will be working with that day. Students fold a paper in four equal parts. The teacher then gives categories for each "box" for the students' closed sort (such as doing words, clothes words, feeling words, and things). The categories given depend upon the words.

Then students independently or with partners sort the words. They write the word in the correct category so this may be assessed later. Students need the writing; please do not have them cut and paste, as the writing reinforces the word knowledge. Also, this way the words can be sorted a different way another day, and the teacher once again gets more with less.

■ Cloze activities: Cloze activities force students to use the context of sentence to fill in the blank. For instance: The man ran up the _____. To increase the complexity of the cloze there could be more than one word to fill in the blank. In the previous example, the answer could be *hill* or *stairs*. For repetition that promotes fluency, use the words from the word sort for a cloze activity on a different day.

■ Specialized words: Contractions, compound words, and more complex words like idioms and euphemisms should be reinforced. If a reading group is reading *Amelia Bedelia 4 Mayor* (Parish 1999), the students can select four idioms from the reading selection, draw the literal meaning, and write a sentence using the idiomatic expression correctly.

Beyond Phonics: Intermediate Activities

Once students have "broken the code" teachers should focus on increasing and expanding student vocabulary. Although students learn most of their vocabulary from wide reading (Armbruster, Lehr, and Osborne 2001), reinforcement expands and clarifies word meaning. I remember when my son, a high school freshman, was trying to gain points on his essay by using impressive vocabulary. He was writing about politics and went to the computer thesaurus to look up a "better" word that would mean the same as saying someone was really, really, good. Somehow, he ended up with the word *delicacy*, a word not used in political circles, although there are a lot of delicate situations in politics.

For clear, concise communication students need a broad vocabulary. We need to focus our vocabulary work on at least these three goals: to clarify and enrich meanings, to increase the volume of known words, and to use word knowledge strategies during independent reading.

Here are a few activities and techniques for word study.

■ Word sorts (yes, again). Let's choose some words from a landforms unit: *source, river, stream, mouth, ocean, lake, tributary, mountain, valley, mesa, cliff, plain, desert, tundra,* and *volcano* to name a few. These could be sorted by: types, where people can live, words associated with water, the desert, temperate climate, and so forth. The words sorted in these categories should be written down for self-assessment and discussion during group time. Word sorts can be done with vocabulary for any narrative or informational text. This technique makes students reread the word, think about the word, and analyze where it might belong and why.

■ Graphic organizers (many can be found with an online search): Have students identify properties of the word, write associations, and write a definition in their own words.

■ Word strategy work can be done by having students use their reading to find words of which they are not clear on the words' meanings. Then, have them guess at the meaning through the use of context.

■ Use the dictionary. Someone has to check to see if the guess that was given for the context clues strategy was correct!

■ Word cards with pictures drawn for an association have been shown to be helpful in getting students to remember word meaning.

Concluding Thoughts

Postreading activities are opportune times to get your students to delve into the meaning of the text or reinforce material. Ideas for postreading activities can sometimes come from the children themselves. They may have an idea to make something from the story that no doubt will be motivating and engaging. The teacher's angle is to also make sure it involves learning and literacy. For instance, when reading *Someone Is Watching* (Patneaude 1993), in which the little sister is thought to be dead, as a solution to looking for the young girl, students may mention that the boys could have made "reward for finding" posters. The group can do this as a response to reading, although they would need to be told what is expected on the poster.

CHAPTER 8

Ensuring Success of Long-Term Projects: Guidelines and Troubleshooting

A glance around Mrs. Hudson's fourth-grade classroom shows students are busy. Two groups are in the planning stages of a mural depicting the events in their current reading book. They explain that Mrs. Hudson will not let them put one pencil mark on the four-foot-long butcher paper until they have planned their mural design and the themed border. Another group is working with Mrs. Hudson, who is thoroughly explaining the vocabulary map students are to complete at the end of the reading group. Yet a third group sits at tables working in partners on a Venn diagram comparing *Sounder* with dogs that they know . . . and they seem to know plenty.

In Mr. Kerrigan's second-grade classroom the students are also obviously engaged in their learning activities. Partnered students are rereading the basal story that the class worked on yesterday. Mr. Kerrigan works with one group with leveled readers purchased from the basal company; this particular unit is themed on pigs. Others are scattered around the room working at various centers. The computer skills game has the students working on the *ig* onset. Another center initially looks like it belongs in a kindergarten room with the plastic barn and farm animals. However, two students are using the farm animals as props in a puppet-type show they are writing. Jeremy and Tyler will perform the puppet show during the next indoor recess, after Mr. Kerrigan has okayed their completed work. Their classmates will donate a nickel to see the puppet show. The money the puppeteers earn will go into a collection and eventually be given to a charity that the students vote on.

Long-term projects are a joy for both the teacher and students. Long-term projects work well with guided reading because they set up the students for independent work for a longer period of time than daily projects. Students can often work independently for days with minimal additional instruction. This frees up teaching time and allows time for project surveillance.

How Long is Long Term?

Long-term projects usually last for a duration of two to four weeks but can be longer, even the length of the school year! The projects selected must be motivating, engaging, and serve a real purpose. Projects, completed while other groups are having guided reading with the teacher, can be done by individuals, partners, groups, contributed to by the whole class, or school. A whole-school project could be as simple as the cutout "shoes" that are often seen lining the hall walls making their way to the principal's office as a visual monument of the amount of books being read by students in the school. This foot-shaped book list is derived from books read during independent time. To get more from less, this project should be modified: make the cutout shoes have cutout feet with exaggerated toes. On the foot have students write the title of the book, the name of the author, and draw a picture of a main character. On the big toe, have the students write the name of a main character, and then have them analyze the character by writing one descriptive word on each of the four other toes. Set up a shoebox of blank feet, and this motivating long-term project can be completed without further direction.

Whether the project is destined to last two weeks or a larger part of the school year, planning and preparation are paramount. Neither has to take an astronomical amount of time. This chapter guides teachers in the development of projects that can be easily implemented during the guided reading block and can be adapted to the curriculum within the school. Successful long-term independent projects have common components that ensure the projects effective implementation and completion.

- The project has to be motivating.

- The project must have substance and reinforce the curriculum.

- The project must be modeled to be successful.

- The project must reinforce needed skills and strategies.

- Materials must be well organized.

- Materials must be available.

- All parts of the assignment must be viable.

- Project rules must be decided and enforced.

- Students must be held accountable for daily progress.

The Project Has to Be Motivating

Although demanding and measuring teacher dispositions in teacher education programs has become a controversial topic, there is one disposition most effective teachers probably have in common: the willingness to do what it takes to help children learn. The willingness to take the extra step to help students often makes a huge difference in their attitude and achievement. Approaching the curricula in a way that makes students want to learn defines motivation. Sometimes, motivation is spread throughout the whole classroom simply by the enthusiasm of the teacher!

I remember vividly when my oldest son came home from school saying he needed paper towel rolls to make a totem pole in school. He was so excited, and I was too. I could picture his first-grade brain contemplating the deeper meanings of totem pole faces and clicking with "aha" moments as he painted and created his own symbols of living. Days later the totem pole arrived home, the crayon-colored ditto paper faces glued so that the brown in the towel roll dominated the product, and the paper wings that were to jut out in Native American pride crunched from its fifteen minutes of life in the backpack. There was no, "Mom, see this!" What could have been a highlight memory for a class of children became another worksheet, this one pasted in the round. A literacy moment was lost forever.

How different that project could have been! Totem poles, emblems of family and family stories, are still carved and painted today. Imagine charts of totem faces and symbols hanging in the classroom; children listening and reading about totem poles, the meanings of the carvings, and the prominence of the totem pole's place in the unity of the tribe; then having students consider their own families (their tribe), no matter the composition, and discussing symbols to represent the unity in their family. Can you visualize young minds thinking about their own families and what facial expressions could portray fun, love, and courage? Or perhaps a family story, one the child needs to tell?

Our totem poles will be two-paper towel rolls high, having four sections, for faces or symbols important to the child. Behind the scenes, two paper towel rolls have been taped together to give bigger height and attached to a piece of cardboard to allow them to stand upright. Paper has been cut so that four pieces can be wrapped completely around the totem pole. Of course, enough of this paper has been cut to allow for mistakes, because mistakes will be made. Students are given a draft paper, a piece of the larger white construction paper folded into four sections to organize their space. Students are ready to draft their own family totem pole. The first graders are told to think about four important facts about their own family, which in this broader sense, and in identifying with Native Americans, would go beyond the immediate family, including cousins, aunts, uncles, and grandparents. In essence, the whole tribe! In each box the students write an important fact about their family and draw the face or symbol that will represent that fact. Once the draft has been accepted, they are ready to make their own family totem pole. In their independent time, students will use watercolor to paint the four sections of the totem pole on the prepared paper. The students would receive help putting these papers onto the totem pole. Fake grass or hay is glued onto the bottom cardboard to cover the tape. What a project of which to be proud, not only for the student but also the teacher. This literacy project goes beyond reading and writing. Through a hands-on experience, these first graders have gained a sense of symbolism.

The primary focus of sample projects offered in the chapter is literacy, but some equally involve other areas of the curriculum. From past reading it seems that many experts expect the literacy block to focus mainly on literacy instructional activities. It is my belief that the integration of other subjects in long-term projects is a viable, natural and often necessary component of the project.

The Project Must Have Substance and Reinforce the Curriculum

Weaving a pot holder is fun and motivating and takes time. Although you may have read a story to the class about students making pot holders, it does not reinforce the language arts curriculum. Long-term projects must be connected academically to the classroom or district's curriculum. Making model cars is also fun and motivating and takes time, and a teacher may argue that it teaches problem-solving skills. But the school board and powers that be most likely will not be impressed. If your goal is to have children use hands-on activities to problem solve, there are ways to bring this directly into the curriculum. In the Newbery Award winner *Dear Mr. Henshaw* (Cleary 1981), the main character puts an alarm on his lunch box because someone is stealing his lunch. The day he does this, no one steals his lunch. He sits in the cafeteria realizing that the only way he can eat his lunch is to set off the alarm. Spinning off this predicament, we can create a literacy-rich problem-solving activity. Students in the *Dear Mr. Henshaw* reading group can be partnered to make two alarms: one that will be activated when the lunch box is opened, and one that can be deactivated before the lunch box is open. Now, we have quite a problem! First, partners will have to state the problem and their proposed solution. Partners would then have to be given the materials to make an alarm and set up with a guideline and criteria for a daily log. The log will have to include labeled diagrams, explanations of successes and failures, and the next steps. If some partners whip through this project, make this a little more challenging. Have these students make an alarm that buzzes and turns on a light at the same time. Once again, the students must complete the daily log. The final project would be the alarm, along with a poster diagramming the alarm and explaining how it works. Besides problem solving, the literacy components involved in this project are: making connections to story meaning, summarizing, stating the problem, setting goals, labeling, diagramming, sequencing, and writing an explanation.

Too often we get caught up in a project that is just fun but doesn't get the learning mileage we need from instruction during the school day. How do you measure substance in a literacy project? We can easily view what substance is not. For instance, classroom teachers often assign word searches. They are motivating and fun. Doing word searches or even making word searches has never been written up as an effective practice. Even though the word search may have the vocabulary of the curriculum, it is not reinforcing learning. Teachers may say that if the definition is given and the student must find the word, then that is reinforcing vocabulary. The problem with this point is that there is no way to know whether the student actually circled the right word with the right meaning . . . we just know they circled all the vocabulary words! There is no substance and a great amount of time is needed to do the word search.

Substance is measured by the direct connection to learning outcomes and the amount of time spent on obtaining these outcomes. It is important that we keep students engaged in new learning and at their optimal speed. A class newspaper, although tangential to the curriculum, would most certainly reinforce very important writing skills and reading skills at the students' individual levels. A class newspaper may be published monthly or biweekly with the majority of it being written by the students. It is a long-term project that can connect to the curriculum in a variety of ways. It will take a series of minilessons to set up the classroom newspaper project successfully. Students will need to understand the criteria of various products in the newspaper. A classroom newspaper can be directly connected to books being read or to life in the classroom. Not all products will be in every published class

Figure 8–1. *Newspaper Products*

Newspaper Product	Connection to Literature (If Desired)
Dear Abby of the literary world	Students write the pleas and the answers to problems of characters in the books they are reading.
Weather report	Students describe the weather in the books they are reading, for example, sunny in *Little House on the Prairie* (Wilder 1935), snow and blizzard conditions in *Far North* (Hobbs 1996).
Upcoming events	Predictions.
News articles	Summaries of chapters or small books.
Society page	Pictures and description of characters, current happenings in books, like a birthday or wedding.
Obituaries	Description of character at their death.
Classified ads or advertisements	Almost every book has a problem. What would the characters need to solve it? Write an advertisement.
Living/travel	Have students investigate a hobby of a book character. Books have such themes as: taking care of pets, gardening, making club houses, making money, or going on a trip somewhere.
Financial	Books like *Alexandra, Who Used to Be Rich Last Sunday* (Viorst 1980), or *Holes* (Sachar 1998) include subtle or blatant details about finances. Many characters could use some financial advice!
Health	Healthy living articles can stem from a variety of character situations. The little brother that eats dirt, the cold, stomachache, the overweight character all give ideas for a health column.
Consumer review	When something goes wrong in a book with an appliance, car, and toy or when a character is saving to buy something new, a consumer review would be warranted.
Editorial/opinion page	Students write their opinion about events in the story. They must support their opinions with facts from the book.

newspaper. A decision needs to be made by comparing what the books being read offer to the type of product that can be created. Some ideas for newspaper columns are described in Figure 8–1.

The Project Must Be Modeled to Be Successful

The gradual release of responsibility cannot be forgotten. When working with guided reading groups, students completing independent work must be confident in what they are doing. Otherwise, chaos ensues. When children completely understand a task at hand, are aware of the expectations, and have had guided practice, they will be able to complete independent tasks successfully.

One long-term project that can be extremely successful or very poorly done is the creation of a comic book to summarize the text being read. Components need to be modeled for the students, and students need to practice with short pieces. Comic books use mainly dialogue to tell a story, and bringing covert action into dialog is a learned skill. Students need to begin with comic strips and as they gain techniques graduate to comic books. Minilessons will need to include: the difference between thought balloons and say balloons, the narrator segment, the print of yelling versus talking, how to show an elapse of time, how to make character speech into comic speech, how to draw pictures that infer how to portray characters' feelings, and how to cut out lengthy sections of a book but maintain the story line. The text structure of comic books should also be explained: the title page, the introduction of characters, and the various lengths of the panels. Once these attributes of comics have been explained and modeled for the students, they should be successful in completing a comic book. (See Appendix 8–1 for a comic page in which students may vary the panel size by drawing in vertical lines.)

The Project Must Reinforce Needed Skills and Strategies

All the projects suggested in this chapter reinforce needed skills and strategies. This reinforcement should take place at all grade levels. One long-term project, an alphabet book, can be created from kindergarten and up. This book can be as simple as an "A is for apple" to reinforce the alphabet to something a little more complicated, like "Q is for Duck" (because it quacks). The upper grades could make an alphabet book Jerry Pallota style. This book would include facts on any informational topic they are currently reading about, such as Native Americans, animals, weather, or electricity, just to name a few areas.

A number of long-term projects involve writing to reinforce the curriculum. Some examples: students can write a radio play to build summarization skills and practice the play to perform, building fluency (Prescott-Griffin and Witherell 2004), and then they can make this into a CD and design its cover; students can write an anthology of poetry depicting the moods and tones in the story line and include illustrations; or they can write and then videotape a commercial to advertise an important event in a story.

Materials Must Be Well Organized

The materials need to be easily accessible, they need to be user-friendly and they need to "fit" what is being done. If all three criteria are not met, life in the fast lane will become life in the breakdown lane. When something frustrates students and they cannot complete the assigned task, trouble happens. It may cause continuous interruptions to your guided reading group, unruly students, and general uncertainty. Even the "good" students, who try to guess what to do, may end up with lots of problems.

Last week I visited a first-grade class where the students were doing a small project with onset and rimes. They were making a t-scope out of *an* words. The teacher gave out a drawing of a pan with the *an* rime printed in the pan. Students were to write the letters *c, f, m, p, r, t* and *v* on the strip. The teacher showed them the model, and they read the word *family* together as she brought the strip of letter through the pan. Two things went wrong: (1) students at this age couldn't understand they were to cut an opening and most sliced through the pan, and (2) although the students could write the requested letters, the size was not guided. So, although students worked independently on this project, the end result was not as intended. Many students had sliced pans with two letters (one on top of the other) in front of the *an* rime. In this case, the teacher should have made the twelve slits (two on each t-scope) for this group of six students and drawn guidelines for the size of the letters. During her directions she should have told students they needed to make their letters as big as the *an* on the pan. These three small organizational ideas would have made a huge difference in this project.

Materials Must Be Available

This sounds so simple; we are teachers after all. We are also human. Long-term projects, such as the feet tally for books read, need to be frequently resupplied. If someone finishes their work earlier than others and seems disengaged, she can be encouraged to read a book and add to the tally in the hall. (Being able to go into the hall and tape up the foot is a motivator. . . .) But, if she reads the book and goes for a foot to find the box empty, things just do not work.

Last year, in a minilesson format I introduced letter writing to a second-grade class and had students write a letter to me on preformatted paper. A rural mailbox was set up, and I explained to students that when they were finished with their seatwork, they could write and "send" a letter to any of their classmates. It was explained that putting up the red flag on the mailbox meant there was mail to be delivered. Formatted paper was left near the mailbox, and an ongoing long-term project had been started. If the classroom teacher did not replenish the formatted paper, this project would lose its viability. However, teaching the next step—the letter friendly format—would solve the supply problem.

Always plan ahead, and keep checking. One method that helps with paper replenishing is the "red tag" approach. Put a red tag of paper in the pile with a corresponding message, such as "The mailbox letter paper needs to be refilled" or "Time to copy off more feet." Tell students that when they get to the red tag they need to hang it in a designated place or put it on your desk. This will give you time to replenish before all is gone and gives the students responsibility.

All Parts of the Assignment Must Be Viable

In our rush to get so much done, we often forget to make sure all will work out. Once in a grade 3 classroom, I was observing the teacher working with a guided reading group. The paraprofessional was working with another group, and students were working independently at their desks. Students who were to be working independently at their desks were noticeably unsettled. They were chattering, getting out of their seats, and in general not accomplishing their work. It did not take long to ascertain the problem. The worksheet given to the students was a strategy sheet, employing questioning as a comprehension technique. The sheet asked students to write questions before they read, while they read, and after they read. Two-thirds of this paper was to be completed prior to the postreading section of their lesson. They had read the story during their guided reading group and truly did not know what to do with the paper. It was not viable. To help with damage control, it was suggested they pretend they had not read the selection yet and to fill in the first two portions. This task kept them quiet and on task while the teacher finished meeting with the current reading group, but any outcome that was to be reached by completing this paper had been lost.

When putting together long-term projects ask "What can go wrong and where?" Answers will come! It is helpful to place a model of a finished project or the expected look of a finished project so students can refer to this. For younger children, picture cues with directions are helpful.

Project Rules Must Be Decided and Enforced

Our focus is learning, but without project rules students forget the importance of the assigned project. Unwanted behaviors can take precedence over the learning. It is best to set up behavioral and academic expectations at the onset of any project. Rules may be as simple as "No more than two people may get materials at the same time" to "At the end of time, you must put your working paper in the folder, and put the folder in the project basket." Rules need to be clearly understood and enforced.

Some long-term projects, such as writing a play based on the story, encourage collaboration. Collaboration with all its pluses easily lends itself to students getting off-task and disrupting others' learning. For group projects, having groups create a schedule or time line of what work will be completed daily will help keep them on task (see next section). In the case of writing and practicing a play, the following rules may help: Use inside voices. Do not talk when others are talking. Do your share. Check your time line to see that your group is where it should be. Be prepared to tell Mrs. X what has been accomplished this work session.

When the rules are not followed, there will need to be some consequences. In the case of the play, students could continue solo on their work the next day—even the practicing. A day or two of this and checking back into the work time line will encourage students to work collaboratively and stay on task!

Students Must Be Held Accountable for Daily Progress

We all know how good children can be at not being accountable. Long-term projects take self-discipline, and students are just learning the art of self-discipline. The more independent the method of accountability is, the easier for the teacher. But teachers know that in the long run, they are responsible for their children's learning. There are various ways that students can be held accountable, including the following.

■ Hand out a teacher-made work time line (schedule) and explain your expectations to the students. (See sample in Figure 8–2.) Periodically check to see they are where they should be.

■ Have students write down where they are in their project each time they work on it by completing a status sheet (Appendix 8–2).

■ Keep time in your schedule for an oral debriefing for group projects. Let them know ahead of time, and do not forget to debrief.

■ For some students, a date for completion is all they need. (If this is the case, consider yourself lucky!)

Keep the project fast-paced. Do not give students time to waste. If the pace is too fast, you will notice as students get behind. If that is the case, adjust the pace accordingly.

Figure 8–2. *Work Session Time Line*

Work Session	What You Must Do
Work session 1	Fill out story map to draft story.
Work session 2	Work on first draft.
Work session 3	Work on first draft.
Work session 4	Finish first draft, peer edit, hand in for teacher input.
Work session 5	Begin second draft.
Work session 6	End second draft, hand in for teacher input.
Work session 7	Decide which lines will be on each page and begin final draft.
Work session 8	Complete final draft.
Work session 9	Work on black drawing outlines.
Work session 10	Work on black drawing outlines, hand in for teacher input. (Teacher should check to see that the drawings match the child's written text.)
Work session 11	Paint illustrations.
Work session 12	Paint illustrations.
Work session 13	Check over entire book, hand in for binding.

In Figure 8-2, the long-term project is to write a piggyback book to *Click, Clack, Moo, Cows That Type* (Cronin 2000). In this book cows go on strike because they want electric blankets. They type a note, which is delivered by duck. Eventually, they get the electric blankets and begin giving milk again. The book's illustrator drew black ink drawings and used watercolor to fill in the drawings. We would expect the students to do this too.

Comic Format

Project Status Sheet

Date	Goal for today—what should get done:	What did get done:	What's next?

CHAPTER 9

Ideas for Independent Long-Term Projects

Have you every walked into a classroom and found groups of children totally engrossed in the task at hand? Chances are they were working on an engaging project, one that had them captivated. You should notice a similar reaction when using exciting long-term projects in your classroom. A number of motivating ideas are offered in this chapter. The time used to set up long-term projects is well worth the time gained. Once the project has been started, well-timed and orchestrated minilessons keep the pace going. The projects can stem from books being read, basal units, or curriculum infusion. The projects reinforce literacy skills taught previously and those being taught in minilessons. They are very much a part of the guided reading block, helping to pave the way to independent readers, writers, and thinkers.

To keep the long-term project going smoothly, it is recommended that the teacher gather updates from the students. This can be done from the status sheet discussed in the previous chapter or from status check-ins done at the beginning or end of the guided reading group time. If you have eight students in a guided reading group, you can gather their status in four minutes or less. If you do this with the whole class, you will need about fifteen minutes to ascertain everyone's status, thereby wasting an additional ten minutes of everyone's time.

This chapter will give ideas for two different types of long-term projects. The first long-term project is one that takes the students two to four weeks to complete. The second is an ongoing project that can be done sporadically or systematically for a long period of time (like the mailbox mentioned in the previous chapter). The ongoing projects exist at various times throughout the year but should take only one or two of the students' independent work blocks to completely understand expectations. After that the ongoing project is an add-on in that once the project has been explained, the teacher can assign the project to coincide with the current curriculum. For example, one ongoing project, a notebook compilation of book recommendations, may be added to at students' will. This becomes an academically based project fostering writing and validating reading to be completed during independent time. In addition, the book review notebook fosters reading and reading choice when students read the recommendations for advice in selecting a new book.

Literacy is the focus of any long-term or ongoing project offered here. The projects may originate from either nonfiction or fiction text. Perhaps students are writing a piggyback book to Eric Carle's *Have You Seen My Cat?* (1987), and they are using paints or markers to replicate a similar artistic style; the focus is on literacy and the interpretation of the illustrator/artist. Or in a similar vein, when students are writing math problems in response to a Greg Tang book, they are working on content area literacy.

The teacher should begin long term-projects with modeling and gradually release the responsibility to the students. Some projects may take longer to explain than others depending on the students' prior knowledge and familiarity with the product. When comparing two of the activities that follow, it will most likely take more explanation for the project on making brochures than for creating games, as students are more familiar with card and board games. Teachers must decide how much preteaching is necessary for students to independently complete the following projects either individually or collaboratively. In addition, the long-term projects used in your classroom should reflect your curriculum, goals, and teaching personality. The wide range of projects offered here can fit with most curricula but may need to be modified.

Brochures

Brochures can be used on any topic and force students to summarize, categorize details, and highlight main ideas. When developing a brochure vocabulary choice is extremely important as the language must be vivid and attract the reader. The purpose of a brochure is to market a product whether this is to advertise a bed and breakfast or to encourage the readers to buy a new phone service. The brochure can "market" the narrative text the students are reading, or an event in the text, or can be purely informational in nature.

It will take at least three minilessons to prepare students to begin their brochure. When modeling the designing of brochures, teachers should use real brochures for concrete examples. The teacher should begin with a minilesson using brochures and have students discover and share the elements they identify in the brochure. Some identifiable elements are: the number of folded sections, the title section, diagrams, maps, pictures, logos, slogans, registration forms, websites, cost tables, directions, objectives, marketing language, calendar of events, list of objects, itineraries, and disclaimers. Along with these elements students should be aware of the design.

The second minilesson should focus on the setup and how the brochure should be created. Using 8½ by 14-inch paper, students can easily fold this three or four times, resulting in six or eight sections counting the front and back of the paper. The elements must be discussed and what is included in each explained. The teacher can decide whether to assign elements or list all elements and require certain elements to be on the brochure.

The third minilesson will share the written criteria and expectations for design and content coverage. These criteria may include: the title section, a certain number of summaries or factual information, a specific range of pictures or diagrams, that grammar and mechanics should be acceptable, and so forth.

One strategy to gain higher-quality end products is to request that students first use sticky notes to show their design or first create a pencil mockup. Either way there should be a checkpoint before the students continue. In this way the teacher can be assured that the students understand what is to be included on the brochure.

A variation: to get more with less, students can use this same information to write and eventually perform a commercial. Again, the criteria must be decided, for example: the length of time for the commercial (no more than sixty seconds), the type (radio or television) the main content, and the selling gimmick. Students need to be made aware of how this commercial should look as a completed project.

Games

Want to motivate students? Tell them they are going to design and construct a game and they will be hooked! The game of course will be totally dependent on literacy experiences. The current reading material will dictate the subject of the game. For ease, it is suggested that games be made to fit in a pizza box (can be created on the pizza cardboard) or in a shoebox. The boxes can be easily stored, stacked, recognized, retrieved, and all the game components will be self-contained.

Once again, there will need to be one or two minilessons prior to the students making the game. As with the brochures, the teacher could use classroom games for modeling and have students describe the components of their home games. There should be a discussion on the type of game they may design. For instance is the game one of luck? strategy? skill? decision making? a combination of types? Will the game need a moderator? Will the game allow one player, two, four? How does someone win? Will the game have a spinner? dice? Does it need markers? And, most importantly what content will it cover? And how will that content be covered? Will it be written on a game board? on cards? a cube? something you throw? The students' imagination will be the limit of this game design. But, the game *must* fit the criteria set up by the teacher.

The main outcome is the learning acquired from the reading, writing, and possible research and the decision making needed to complete this long-term project. (A secondary outcome occurs when classmates learn from playing the game.) Explain the criteria of the game in a minilesson prior to this project being started. The criteria, selected by the teacher and perhaps the students, may include such things as: a name, a cover design for the box, all required game components, acceptable grammar and mechanics, clear directions, list of components and the number of pieces, focus on content, and a justification explaining how the game reinforces the content.

Diary of a Character

Understanding a character's feelings, motivations, interactions, and relationships with others is essential in gaining deep understanding of a character and a character's connection to the plot. When students write a diary in the role of the character, they develop an appreciation for how the character feels and why, along with insights in response to the character's action. One minilesson modeling a character entry from one chapter or a picture book might be all the students need to understand this project. For motivation, students can make small four- by five-inch diaries by stapling paper together and gluing on ribbon to tie the diary shut. Younger children can use a shape book, such as a turtle if they are writing the diary of Franklin.

Students who are reading chapter books can write the diary chapter by chapter. Students reading picture books should do this with series books because series books, such as Curious George and Arthur, allow students to become very familiar with the character. As in all projects, the criteria must be specific. In writing a character's diary students should begin with the greeting and the date, which may be made up but within chronological sequence. For instance, if a chapter starts a week later than the previous chapter ended, then this must be noted. Also the diary may include: the

Figure 9–1. *Students Working on Research Projects*

character's feelings, support for those feelings by referring to incidents that occurred in the story, thoughts, physical descriptions of place, weather, other characters and objects, and when appropriate, the character's inferred reaction.

To put a spin on the diary of a character project, the book *Diary of a Worm* (Cronin 2003) makes an excellent model for animal characters. In this amusing book a worm writes a dated diary about school, not having to take baths, and scaring girls. Students can take the role of an animal or insect, such as the spider, Charlotte, in *Charlotte's Web* (White 1952) and write actual incidents with a humorous spider-view twist.

Research Projects: Independent Investigations

Research projects have a bad press because they can involve intense hours with students trying to select, organize, and summarize new information. It does not need to be this way. An independent investigation is motivating, encourages self-learning, and is rewarding. When students complete a research project independently, we want to keep the integrity of the process but break it down into small manageable bites. Minilessons will need to focus on narrowing the topic, components to be included, how the research is to be organized, determining importance to aid in synthesizing texts read, and various research skills, such as skimming for information and documenting resources.

To help students organize their research project, have them begin with a question. Model how to skim for information and to take notes related to this question. Have a minilesson showing how to distinguish interesting from important for note taking. Give students a list of what you expect to be included in the research. Have them decide what the end product will be.

The research project is a coat of many colors. The end product may be: a research paper, a well-designed poster board for display, a Power-Point presentation, a time line, an oral presentation with transparencies, a file or box filled with particular components, or even a paper box covered with well-designed information to serve as a three-dimensional poster. This end product can be assigned or left for student choice. Also, the topic of a research project can be an open topic, in which the students have relatively free rein in deciding what to research. The teacher may mandate the broad topic of the research; although students have less choice, it is still wide enough that students feel they are vested in the project. For instance, the broad topic could be space, but students would select a narrow piece of the topic such as the Milky Way, planets, the sun, asteroids, or spaceships.

If the teacher selects a broad topic, ample resources on the topic can be gathered and made easily accessible. Following is a small sampling of ideas for broad topics: colonial times, civil rights, Olympics, sports, inventions, medicine, fashion, animals, plants, music, ecology, endangered species, world customs and traditions, immigration, industrial age, Middle Ages, technology, survival, making a difference. If books being currently used in the class suggest a broad theme such as friendship or relationships, families, careers, history, art, or such, connecting to the theme would enhance the literacy experience. In addition, the research theme could focus on a future theme to be explored in the classroom and used as a vehicle to build background.

Once the theme or topic has been decided, organizational logistics must be put in place. A time line for the project needs to be developed. The teacher needs to limit the product being developed, meaning whether students may be allowed to have a choice of completing a research paper, a poster display, box report, or some other creative end product. Criteria that fit all products need to be clearly written and shared with the students.

Criteria can be easily selected from the following suggestions: title, an introduction and conclusion for the topic, five to eight significant pieces of information about the topic, an overview such as a table of contents, index cards demonstrating process, visual aids, references, and so forth.

Weighted Projects

Weighted projects are motivating because of the choice and creativity the projects allow students. The process is more easily understood by students in second grade or higher. The weighted project consists of a number of components, with weighted value. The students may choose what components go into the final product. Any projects mentioned in this book can become a part of or the main focus in a weighted project.

As an example, I will use the creation of a storybook home page poster. The finished product is not an actual home page (or website) on the computer, but a design of one, and can offer links for more information (which is posted on back of the poster, or in a flip cutout form). Home pages or websites can be used as models. Some criteria for a storybook home page poster might be: the title; two main topics, two paragraphs in length; six to eight sidebar topics, two sentences in length; up to two advertisements (related to the story); one main picture; two minor pictures; sections designed in the web page view; menu items; and links (more information, approximately three to four paragraphs in length). The items on the home page may be weighed by a given number of points and students may combine as many items as they like, but must have a total of at least fifteen points. (See Figure 9–1.) This means that not all items are mandatory. In this particular project, two items—the title and author and the section design— are stated as "must have." The design of the rest of the web page can be a combination of any of the other components as long they total up to the other twelve points (mandatory points were: two for the section design, and one for author and title). Some enthusiastic students will total much more than fifteen points, but setting the expectation of fifteen points will help control the time length of this project.

Time Lines

Time lines can be done on historical content, story sequence, or chronological order processes such as the life cycle of a butterfly. For instance, the story of *Uncle Jed's Barbershop* (Mitchell 1993) takes place in the segregated south and begins in the 1920s. It is a story of Sarah's Uncle Jed, who temporarily gives up his dream of obtaining his own barbershop as he uses his life savings to pay for Sarah's medical expenses. Then come the struggles of the depression where he loses his savings in the bank. Eventually at the age of seventy-nine Uncle Jed realizes his dream. It is a beautiful story of love and dreams. For younger children, the sequence of the story would work for the time line;

Figure 9–2. *Weighted Project: Storybook Home Page Poster*

Items to Be Included	Description	Points Awarded
Title and author—must have	Write title and author	One point (must have)
Main topics (up to two)	Two main incidents from book, two paragraphs in length	Two points for each
Six to eight sidebar topics	Smaller incidents or events in book, must be two sentences in length	One point for each
One main picture	Picture depicts major story elements or events	Two points
One to three minor pictures	Picture depicts minor events or elements	One point each
Section design—must have	Design and presentation of material, mechanics, and neatness	Two points (must have)
One to two advertisements	Advertises something in or needed in the story	One point each
Menu items (four to eight)	Do not have to have links, but can be a list of characters, setting, or events	One point for whole list
Links	Can be to any component on the web page, must be two to three paragraphs in length and tell more about the topic	Two points per link

With the exception of the two must-have criteria (title and section design), students may choose components as long as they total up to at least fifteen points.

for older students, independently acquired details from the 1920s, the poverty of the 1930s, and so forth should be inserted at appropriate times, adding to their layers of comprehension and to their knowledge of history with such topics as sharecroppers, the depression, and segregation.

Time lines can be made on rolled paper. Capable students could use a software program, such as Timeliner. Criteria and checkpoints need to be set up. Criteria for a time line may include: dates or ages (if given), the initiating event, sequence of events, titles of each event, a short written description, special news of the times, and the story resolution. Approximate dates should be given with all historical events. In the case of chronological sequences, such as the life cycle of a butterfly, the approximate time length should be included.

Writing and Making Books

I could not begin to name all the types of books that could be made for longterm projects. Any of the types mentioned in this chapter can be used for narrative or informational writing. They can be completed independently or collaboratively. For instance, in the alphabet book, students in a group can be assigned particular letters, and the whole book can be stapled together. Each book should require a draft prior to being put on the finished product material. The following ideas stem off of piggyback books but go into more detail in the explanation.

General Books

By general books, I am talking any genre, for instance, story, folktale, fairy tale, mystery, cumulative story, biography, superhero, nonfiction, or even science fiction. Any genre that students have been exposed to and that interests them can be made into books that they write, but criteria must be set. Elements that form a specific narrative genre, for instance, the once upon a time, happily ever after, and magic in fairy tales, along with characters, setting, problem, attempts to solve, and the solution should be included. Also the chapter headings, the resolution, and pictures may be included. A nonfiction book may include: the text, table of contents, visual aids such as graphs and maps, captions, bold headings, index, and glossary.

Alphabet Books

Alphabet books, mentioned earlier, may have anything as a topic, can be fiction or nonfiction, and usually are formatted one page per letter, which works well. For a long-term project that goes deeper into text meeting students could create an alphabet book as a response to *Superfudge* (Blume 1980). Each page would describe an incident or item from the book, in this case: *A* could be for *angry*, as Mom gets very angry when Fudge hides the new baby in the closet; *B* could be for *baby,* as Peter finds out in the first chapter that his parents are expecting another baby, and he does not want another Fudge, and Fudge can't stop talking about the baby; *C* could be for *catastrophes*, which is the name of one of the chapters, and plenty of catastrophes happen in the book.

In the case of a nonfiction alphabet book, any of Jerry Pollotta's ABC books such as *The Icky Bug Alphabet Book* (Pallotta 2000) would make a great model. The students use words or phrases beginning with each letter of the alphabet to write facts about their chosen topic or about the informational text they have read. Criteria would need to be explained for the page setup: the alphabet word or phrase in bigger letters, with an explanation and picture to accompany each page. Side notes may be required.

Magic School Bus Formula

As crazy as the pages appear to adults, children love the *Magic School Bus* (Cole 1969) formula and the page setup, and the good news is Mrs. Fritz can go anywhere. Any Magic School Bus book can be a model, and the more books you use, the better students will understand the model. Teachers should have students read these books and decide the criteria for their own books. This book formula has three basic story line or book section components on each page: the story of the school children, the factual information being presented, and the notes taken by the children that highlight or support the informational material. As a long-term project this is quite an undertaking and is best done in partners. The students should finish the factual information first, and there should be a checkpoint here. Encourage students to use the story children's "notes" as the draft for their factual information. Then the writers can go back and fill in the classroom story line.

Accordion Books

Accordion books can be used for narrative or nonfiction material. Accordion books are books that can be folded up like an accordion, so in essence the pages are folded sections of paper inside the two ends. The pages of an accordion book do not turn but go straight out in sequence, and both front and back can be used. In some ways this simplifies the book process for younger children because it is like using different pages for each piece of the book. Using an accordion book to write a summary of a larger book can be scaffolded for students as the teacher guides what goes on each of the pages. For instance, page 1 may be the summary of pages 1 to 3 in a picture book, or each page may represent a chapter summary from a chapter book. Once again, criteria for each page must be set up and may include some of the following when writing a summary: pictures portraying the actions and/or feelings, summary statements, quotes from the pages or chapter, any other pertinent information from the book.

Flap Books

It is harder to describe how to make flap books than it is to make them. To make a flap book, two pieces of paper are folded over once at different lengths. For instance, an eighteen-inch piece of paper would be folded down at the four-inch mark. Another eighteen-inch piece of paper would be folded at the eight-inch mark. The second paper would then be inserted inside the first paper and both pieces stapled together. You would have a "book" with four flaps, all ending at different lengths. The book can be written to open up from the top or sideways like a traditional book. Each flap may be required to have certain information (and can be used as a report product) or may simply sequence a story. Both sides, with the exception of the very back flap, may be written or drawn on.

Wordless Books

Wordless books are books in which pictures tell the story. An excellent model is *Good Dog, Carl* (Day 1986). In this wordless book a dog is told by the mother of the family to watch the baby as she leaves for work, and from those words this delightful story goes completely wordless. The baby has a great day and all kinds of exciting adventures, including a bath in the fish tank. Eventually mother comes home to a calm, clean house. Students may write their own wordless books or retell a story or book they have read by drawing all the information in pictures. Wordless books are not easy. Three items are extremely important: sequence, details in the drawings, and inferences made from the pictures. The only information a reader gathers is from the pictures and inferences made from prior knowledge. Students need to understand this. For instance, a student may begin a book by drawing a picture of a bird flying away, but if that bird has a cat jumping up or on a nearby tree, the reader infers a completely different meaning.

Comic Books

Although students can write their own original comic books, writing a comic book to retell a story or book read is more than just a summary or retelling of the story. Students need to visualize all-important events and often write dialogue or thought where they might not exist in the original story. In this process at least four comprehension strategies are being used: summarization, visualization, questioning (what might the character be saying or thinking), and making inferences.

Most students will not need modeling of a comic book, but they are readily available. Inside *Moxie Day, The Prankster* (Pottle 2005) is the Poetry Bug

Comic. In this book of poetry and comics, the comic story line has Murphy (Moxie's older brother) trying to deal with Moxie's pranks. The book also includes an informational comic explaining different types of poetry.

When beginning the comic project it is important to give students space with their comic books by folding 8½ by 11-inch plain white paper into four sections. When students try to write dialogue in smaller boxes, it gets very difficult and often illegible. The criteria must be set and may include: a title, author and illustrator names, all important story or factual events, thought and speech balloons, simplified dialogue in most boxes but not necessarily all, exaggerations for humor, an introduction, and a conclusion.

Autobiography

An autobiography as an independent project can be done in a number of ways, simplified for younger students, made much more complex for older students. This may be done in regular book format, as a time line, or as an accordion book. An accordion book is a great pick for younger students. They can be given a book with six to eight sections (three or four on front and back), told to put a title, use each section for their age sequence starting with birth, and then told to draw a picture and write sentences about one event in each year of their life. No matter what the age of the students, they should do their prewriting by talking over age events with others in their life. The criteria for an autobiography can differ but here are some items that have been included: title, sequence of years, place born, schooling, interests during different times of their life (American Girls, PlayStation XX), sporting events, major life issues, and where they are now. An autobiography can be made more challenging for older students by having them include major historical or pop events that occurred during each year of their life.

Class Museums

As long as the artifacts are changed often, classroom museums are a motivating and engaging project. Museums can be a display for anything. There are museums on everything from dolls to shoes to beer cans, which just shows that your classroom museum can highlight anything (legal)! The museum theme can come from any experience, the materials may be real objects or created works of art. Focusing on the museum as a literacy experience means the theme and materials must be changed often. No gathering dust in the class museum!

Index cards must be available so students can write details about the object they plan to display in the class museum. Museum cards usually name the object in large or dark print and give a short description, any dates important to the object, the date the object was placed, and names the lender. Sometimes there is a larger text explaining the whole theme of the exhibit. (Museums can also be highlighted in a class newspaper and can have special events.)

Museums can get their themes from content units or from books. For example, *Click, Clack, Moo, Cows That Type* (Cronin 2000), *Dora's Eggs* (Sykes 1997), and *Sarah, Plain and Tall* (MacLachlan 1985) would lend themselves to a museum on farm animals and equipment (real or toys). The book *Rocks in His Head* (Hurst 2001) would definitely spur a collection of rocks. Or something just plain fun, such as *Aunt Flossie's Hats (and Crab Cakes Later)* (Howard 1991) or *Caps for Sale* (Slobodkina 1968), could be a great spin-off for starting a museum of hats and caps of all kinds.

Plays and Puppet Shows

Plays and puppet shows can be created as an original, as a sequel, or as a retelling of the story or just a chapter. The play or puppet show must be written first, then practiced, and eventually performed. The writing will strengthen vocabulary and encoding skills and the practice will build fluency. Frequent checkpoints are needed when children are writing plays or puppet shows. Minilessons need to provide the format. Materials need to be available for costumes or for making puppets. The "stage" can be a small area of the room; the puppet stage can be behind a table. Scenery for either can be simple.

Books that lend themselves to being made into a play or puppet show should have lots of dialogue. Students must use expression to convey meaning as they speak their parts. Because this is an independent activity, it is recommended that two or three students work in a collaborative group. This limits the book choice but not the theme. *The Greedy Man in the Moon* (Rossiter 1994) would only need three people. This is the story of a man punished for his greed and a boy who is rewarded for his kindness. A play written from *The Bracelet* (Uchida 1993), a warm story of two girls being separated in World War II because one was sent to a Japanese internment camp, could be written with just the two main characters in dialogue. For older students, the fifth chapter in *Bud, Not Buddy* (Curtis 1999) has Bud pretending to talk to his mother (who is no longer living). Two students portraying this chapter in a short play might help others understand the poignancy of this encounter through expression and gestures.

Poster Displays

Poster displays can focus on the topic of informational text or the theme and events in a narrative story. A teacher must decide what needs to be on the poster and what minilessons are needed to ensure students understand the criteria. Criteria on a nonfiction book might be: title, sections including the what, samples, explanation, and visual aids. Narrative posters could include: title and author, the story elements, pictures, opinions, favorite parts, symbolisms and connections. The poster could have a three-dimensional element or scrapbook-like elements. When students have completed their poster, a poster session should be held. Approximately six students at a time will share their poster, and groups of students walk around, admiring and asking questions. This allows for much more participation and dialogue than just sharing in front of the room.

Science Experiments

I am a big believer in using content to teach reading. With the right books and materials, students can basically teach themselves some rudiments of science. As an example, electricity is a topic that can easily become a self-exploratory unit. Students are given wire, batteries, a light or two, a magnet, and any other small items to help complete an electrical experiment. Students need to be given a lab sheet and a minilesson or two modeling how these independent labs should be completed and how the lab reports should look. Multiple books should be available on the topic. Experiments that are easy to follow and understand should be available for the students. They need to be well paced and there must be checkpoints to ensure the students are writing their lab reports. A teacher may offer directions for ten simple electrical experiments. The lab report should contain room for the topic, a hypothesis, steps in the experiment, a labeled diagram of the experiment, and the results. Depending on the level of experiments, students may be expected to do seven of the ten experiments and have the lab reports completed in two to three weeks. Two suggested checkpoints: first lab report to see that it is done correctly, and then the fourth report to check on pacing.

Artistic Renditions

Infusing the arts into the curriculum increases comprehension for many learners (Witherell 2000). Drama (perhaps monologues; see earlier for

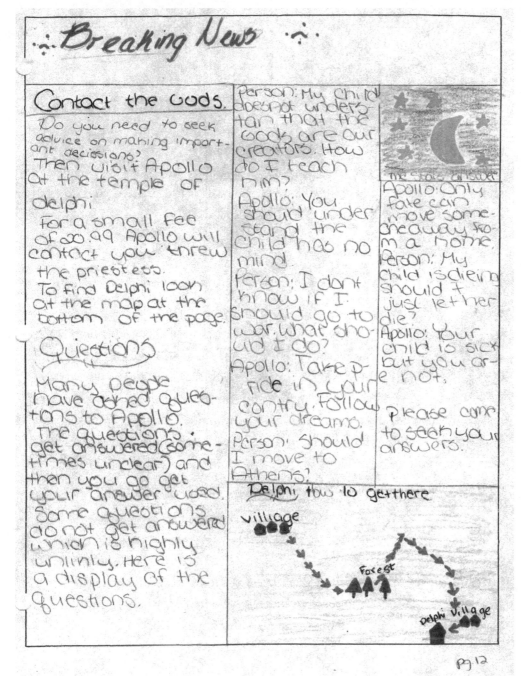

Figure 9–3. *Student Newspaper Sample*

plays), songs, art, and dance can all be used to interpret understanding of a story. Students, in song, can summarize important points, share the mood of the story, and share the deeper meanings of the plot through repetition and tone. Dance can allow students to symbolize events and themes of literature. Students can write their interpretations; while a small number of students dance, the emcee can guide the audience through the interpretation.

The visual arts also allow students to bring their own meaning to the text and the response to the text. A sculpture can symbolize the theme. A chalk drawing or watercolor can portray the various settings. (Teaching tip: Use hairspray over chalk to keep from smudging.) A collage can share events, and the colors chosen can symbolize mood.

When allowing students to use artistic renditions, rules must be set. It may be that the teacher will only allow one group during each book do an artistic rendition. This would control the level of excitement in the room and allow easier coverage of the checkpoints as only one group at a time has to show their progress on this project. At the end of the project there needs to be a sharing. All end products need an audience!

Newspapers

Students can a write a newspaper on any time period or events in a story. The idea here is different from a class newspaper, as this could be made-up articles using information from the book and the history of the era in which the story occurs. In this case, more reading is done as students research possible news items. Newspapers can be collaborative projects in which different children write different areas of the newspaper. As an example, a sixth-grade class, studying Egypt, produced a daily paper highlighting news of the era of the reading. (See Figure 9-3.)

Story Road Map

A story road map can be made on a poster board or time line paper. The purpose of a story road map is to have students recall information in the story, write a summary of events, give the events in sequence, and use visualization in the retelling. In a minilesson, the story road map should be explained and modeled with a simple chalk drawing. It is a map with roads that take viewers through the story by following the main road. As with any good map, it needs a legend to explain symbols used. Students draw and write about events in the story and they make the road connect to these drawings. More sophisticated story road maps may have a U or loop in the road as the main character veers off on a side plot and then returns to the main road.

For students' first attempt at creating a story road map, it is recommended that the teacher should explicitly state (in writing for a long-term project) the events to be included. Students are then given freedom to visualize their own interpretation and summarize the events. They should be encouraged to add interesting details on the route and make up a legend that has key symbols that fit with their interpretation of the book.

Ongoing Projects

Ongoing projects are ones that the teacher begins and can be done at any time throughout the year. They can be themed with units or school celebrations. The goal is to have the project setup done in one lesson, and it takes off from there.

Unique Word Walls

The development of vocabulary and language is a crucial part of literacy. When students do not understand words, idioms, or figures of speech—when context clues fail a student—there is serious interference with comprehension. This is most severe with English language learners. Idioms, euphemisms, similes, and metaphors all fall in this category and need extra teaching to aid in comprehension and ownership of the meaning. The literacy devices mean:

- *Idiom:* A manner of speaking that is natural to native speakers of a language. An example: "rocks in his head" means a person is not too smart.

- *Euphemism:* The substitution of a vague expression to mean something else. An example: using *expecting* for *pregnant*

- *Metaphor:* Comparing two unlike things using the verb *to be* and not using *like* or *as*. An example: The river was a huge snake separating the cliffs.

- *Simile:* Comparing two unlike things using *like* and *as*. An example: The baby is as small as a peanut.

Students should be given minilessons on each of these terms and begin a yearlong scavenger hunt for these types of words or phrases. With each collection the word or phrases should be discussed and applied to ensure understanding. The word wall should display the word and the definition for idioms and euphemisms. In this way, the word wall will continue to be a resource to aid in understanding these terms. Similes and metaphors can be written as found in the book.

Literacy Calendar

A literacy calendar highlights books and characters encountered throughout a few months in school. Months of the year are copied and stapled to a half sheet of poster board. (Later, holes can be punched and ribbon inserted to hang the calendar.) Students decorate around the calendar pages and create their literacy calendar. As students read, they decide what drawings, graphics, and quotes they would like to put on their calendar for decoration. When the calendar pages are surrounded with literacy events, the calendars go home.

Map Work

Geography should be a part of daily classroom activities. We can add to our students' knowledge in geography by keeping a record of what countries and states students visit in their reading. Using a wall map the students mark the spot with a numbered label, which matches a numbered index card that will be put up around the map. Students use the index card to write the book title and explain how the marked country or state contributes to the book. This can be done with whole-class shared books, guided reading books, and independent reading books.

Character Quilt

This ongoing project is another class project that can be worked on for few months or longer. A form (see Appendix 9–1) modeled during a minilesson simplifies this project. Students choose a character they had strong feelings about. Students write the name of the character and the title of the book, and draw a picture of the character as visualized by the student. Finally, the student finishes the statement on the form that reads, "I chose this character because . . ." The finished products are hung on the wall in quiltlike fashion.

Vocabulary Enrichment

Vocabulary, one of the focus areas of the Put Reading First initiative, is back in the limelight—where it should be. The more exact a student's vocabulary, the better she will be able to communicate. Vocabulary enrichment can be aided by some postreading activities to help in the retention of words and word meanings. Word banks should not stop in grade 1. They should continue to be used and to demand more complex thought processes of the student. The main goal of word boxes in grades 1 and 2 is word recognition. Most of the words students encounter in grade 1 they have heard orally. They are given words in their word box to practice and build fluency. Students in these grades should be keeping word boxes and reading these words to a partner during the independent work time. As children get into the upper grades, word boxes need to have more information. The index card should have the word and a student-made picture on the front for meaning association. On the back students should write a definition of the word in their own words and put the word in a phrase that helps them recall meaning. The words in the boxes are then practiced with partners, where the word is read and a sentence is given. Student word retention improves with multiple exposures and use of new words.

Concluding Thoughts

Deciding what long-term projects your class can complete has, in some ways, the same considerations as using centers. If writing a play or puppet show is one of your long-term projects, you must be able to tolerate students practicing while you are meeting with a reading group. Your room must be long enough, or another space, with perhaps a parent volunteer, must be available for practice. If your students are making a four-foot-long mural, there must be table, wall, or floor space, enough for the mural paper and the students. The advantage of long-term projects outweigh any disadvantages, and in the end the students doing the long-term projects and the students in the uninterrupted reading groups are the winners.

Character's Name _____

Book Title _____

Picture:

I chose this character because

CHAPTER 10

Minilessons for Center Preparation

Centers are something a teacher either loves or loves to hate. Keeping centers "kid ready" can be an arduous task; classroom management in both student behavior and logistics can be a trying experience; and finally, accountability can be a principal's nightmare. There are number of positive reasons why children should be allowed the use of centers. Centers:

- are motivating and engaging for students

- can reinforce skills and strategies taught in minilessons, guided reading, and shared reading

- can reinforce or extend content area learning

- allow space for topics tangent to the curriculum

- can be designed to meet the needs of all learners

- force students to take partial responsibility for their own learning

- scaffold students into independent learning

- provide an interactive change of pace (Farris, Fuhler, and Walther 2004)

There are many more pluses to utilizing centers than minuses. When making the decision to use centers in the classroom, the teacher needs to proceed slowly to ensure students understand the purpose and tasks at each center and the expectations during center time. Once a classroom has an effective "center mentality," it is amazing what students can do. Students need to be scaffolded for independent work to guarantee success and to ensure they understand all expectations.

Should I or Should I Not?

When making the decision to use centers and determining the type of centers in the classroom, a teacher needs to consider the environment, the needs and abilities of the students, and what specific curriculum facets are best served in this medium. In addition, the teacher needs to greatly consider her own tolerance for conversation and movement within the classroom while she is meeting with reading groups.

On the other hand, the advantages of centers should also be considered. Once students understand the rules, centers are easily used. Centers allow teachers uninterrupted time with their reading groups. Most centers are easy to maintain. And finally, students enjoy centers and are engaged in the learning.

The Types of Centers

As mentioned earlier, there are three types of centers: stationary, portable, and cruise. Centers, such as one for writing or a reading area, can be stationary. Shoebox centers, which are located on the shelf and brought to the children's desk, are portable centers. Finally, there are cruise centers, where children walk around the room pursuing an academically minded project. Each of the centers is set up differently, and specific components within the center keep students on task and responsible. Teachers may consider using one type of center or a combination of two or three types in their classroom. Although specific center ideas will be included in the next two chapters, understanding of the types of centers is important here.

Stationary Centers

Stationary centers stay where the teacher decides to put them and do take up space. Good stationary centers are well organized and equipped. They look appealing, and they motivate learning. The teacher must decide the number of students that should be allowed to work at the center at one time, how to best organize the required materials for the work to be done, and how this work will be submitted. Space is important at the center as crowded students are less apt to remain peaceful.

Portable Centers

Portable centers are easily stored in plastic shoeboxes or pizza boxes. Although you may use larger boxes, they obviously take more space, which

Figure 10–1. *Cruise Centers: Ready to Measure*

is often premium in the classroom. It is best not to have things too big because centers are often changed. (Most centers need to be stored twice, they need an area when available for use, and then a spot to be put away to be used another time.) The portable center has everything the student needs right inside the container. For instance, if students need a white board marker, keep it in the storage container. The center is designed for "one-stop shopping." It is not efficient for students to roam the room to gather needed supplies. Portable centers can be on any curriculum topic; they are simply different packaging.

Cruise Centers

Fountas and Pinnell (1996) refer to "read the room" centers; I call them cruise centers. Students roam or cruise the room with an academic mind-set, reading the environment and reinforcing classroom curriculum. As students cruise, they study the word wall and white boards; manipulate pocket charts; read other students' writing, posted poetry, and anything else that is labeled in the room. Cruise centers, a name appreciated by older students, reinforce curriculum in various ways and allow students to revisit bulletin boards, read student papers on display, or rearrange those cute little magnetic words into a winning poem.

Considerations for Centers

Consider the Environment

Not all classrooms are created equal. When deciding whether to use centers and what type of centers to use, classroom size, shape, and build need to be considered. In open-space classrooms or rooms with thin movable walls, teachers need to be cognizant of the centers' effect on neighboring classes. There are basically three types of centers: stationary (stays in place at a table, desk, or floor area), portable centers (container centers that students take to their work area), and cruise centers (students roam the room with a particular academic task). If a teacher has thirty-four students in a small room, a large number of stationary centers may be detrimental. In this case, it might be best to have one or two stationary centers and a number of shoebox centers. In contrast, if the teacher has a large room and the classroom is not crowded, a large number of stationary centers could be opportune. The cruise centers could be used in either case, as long as the number of students moving at one time is limited to fit the smaller room.

When thinking about what centers to use and the classroom layout, teachers should consider the traffic pattern of the students (Owocki 2005). Students should be able to move freely from where they sit to the centers. Graph paper can be used to figure out the space needed. Cut small rectangles and squares to approximate the size of classroom furniture. Large chart graph paper is ideal for considering layout (usually one inch equals one foot). The pieces are easily moved and labeled and you get a much better feel for how things will fit. Simply approximate the size, and when you notice objects are two squares from each other, ask yourself if that is enough space.

When thinking about space, think of the students' size and needs. Two feet is plenty of space for most six-year-olds to pass through, not for sixth graders. Also consider that for some students and tasks assigned, a quiet space will be more advantageous for the completion of the work. The classroom should have a work area away from the centers as center activity for these students could be distracting.

Consider the Students

When designing centers, teachers need to decide what can be expected of their students academically, socially, and physically. Centers need to be differentiated in abilities either through open-ended responses/products or tiered activities. All students need to be able to be successful with center tasks. Frustrated students do not learn, and this affects other aspects of the classroom. On the other hand, centers offer great opportunity to challenge the gifted students and help teachers fill a void in meeting the needs of students who need to apply themselves to more difficult tasks in particular content areas.

Although we want focused discussion at centers, the social characteristics of the students must be heavily considered. If a teacher plans on using stationary centers, she needs to consider the number of students to allow at each center. Can the classmates work peacefully and effectively with as many as four or five? Or would it be better to limit the number to two? Some centers, like the writing center, may work well with as many as six, but the computer center with one computer should probably be limited to two.

Even with shoebox centers, questions must be asked. Can the students use the shoebox center at their work area? The teacher must ask how he can ensure students will get and return the center to its location and not end up in trouble. Can students be responsible with the components of the center? How many students does the teacher want using the shoebox center at one time?

Next the teacher needs to consider any physical limitations that students in the class may have. At stationary centers, objects need to be low enough and near enough for everyone to reach. Some questions to consider: If necessary, is the center wheelchair accessible? Do some children need bigger print? Do the centers have manipulatives usable by all children?

Centers must be childproof and ready, whether you are working with first grade or fifth. I remember when my nine-year old niece had an infection in her nose. The young fourth grader went around in pain for three days, until she finally admitted to her mother she had a small eraser from her pencil stuck in her nose. One quick trip to the hospital took it out. The lesson here: We need to think about what could go wrong, even if we think our students are old enough to know better.

Minilessons: Preparing Students for Centers

No matter what type of center the students are using, it is extremely important that students understand the tasks at a center. Minilessons explaining and modeling the expectations of a center can ensure students understand. A minilesson for center activities can focus on the complete center or an aspect of a center. The teacher needs to decide what children need to know to do the center activities successfully. For instance, although most students are software savvy, a computer center would still need explanation as there are ins and outs of almost any software program. If students are made familiar with these, the center time will go much more smoothly.

For emergent readers, the software program may be as simple as using a game format to reinforce letter identification. A web search on "letter identification computer games for beginning readers" resulted in a number of free on-line games. One game, with good ol' Clifford, involved putting *p* and *b* words into the correct box. Simply done, the students drag the word into the box. Headphones would be recommended as the word was said orally when placed in the box, which of course helps with their word identification skills. Once the students finish filling the boxes with the correct words, there is an option to print the results (hence accountability and assessment to guide the next computer activity). The purpose of this activity is to help students differentiate between the letters *p* and *b* and to increase their sight vocabulary.

But let's talk about before. Students would need a minilesson to prepare them for the skills at this center. For instance, the teacher would show the two letters *p* and *b*. She would then talk about the letter sound, such as *p* as in *pet* and *b* as in *bat*. She would then ask for students to give words that begin with the letter *b* and list them on the board, underlining the letter and bringing attention to the fact that the *b* is tall. She would do the same with *p* words, bringing to attention that like most pets, the letter *p* has a tail. Once this has been taught to the children, the computer program would reinforce these differences.

Another short minilesson would introduce the computer program. Students simply need to watch the teacher play and be told to hold the mouse button when they drag the word over. In this case, they should be directed to print when done, put their name on the paper, and place it in the in box. With young children, it is best to open the program for them and have it ready at center time.

For older students searching under the topic "vocabulary games for children" brought up a number of free games. One game, Vocabulary Pinball, allowed teachers to insert their own words. The player plays pinball and spells a vocabulary word through direct hits. Once the word has been spelled, the player chooses the correct definition. Once again, headsets would be recommended, as the pinball sound, which is initially amusing, wears thin.

In this case, the minilesson would focus on the vocabulary words being spelled in the game. Teachers would need to show students how to play this game with a number of the words. Once a word has been spelled, the meaning should be discussed and the word modeled in a sentence. For accountability students should write down the spelled words, and use, say, five of them in a sentence. If the program is bookmarked under favorites, older students can open this program on their own. Word games on-line have many advantages: they are free, they are varied, and the majority of students can continue to play them at home or at a local library—and they do!

Just Right Reading Center

A free-choice reading center can easily be introduced but does need a minilesson for the most effective center use. In guided reading groups, the teacher should use as a minilesson topic how students decide when a book is just right and actually have students practice choosing just right books. First, the teacher should orally explain how to choose the just right book. Then using a selection of books with the guided reading group, students practice choosing by partner reading. Together the partners can decide if the book is just right, too easy, or too hard. Once partners have correctly chosen a least three books, the teacher can assume the students understand the process. Some teachers, to make choices simpler for students, offer baskets of books at the reading center that have been previously leveled for the reading groups. This is a great idea, but students still need to be able to pick out their own just right books.

A reading center can be stationary or mobile. If a teacher prefers, students can be told they must select a few books and return to their desk. This loses the motivation of getting to read someplace "neat," and allowing the students a change of pace. Our goal is to get students to love to have reading center time, and having a huge selection of books and comfy reading areas can do this. Reading center areas have been designed in some very creative ways, using futons, beanbag chairs, small tents, small plastic swimming pools, lofts, and even antique four-legged bathtubs, painted in stripes, of course.

Writing Center Minilessons

Most centers will be introduced with minilessons to the whole class. Sometimes, as mentioned previously, this can be done in one short minilesson. At other times, a series of lessons will be needed to assist students in producing high-caliber work at the centers. The writing center can offer a myriad of products, and each would need at least one minilesson. As an example we can use a fun theme: creating concoctions. The teacher chooses books that have mixtures or crazy formulas as a focus. One choice may be *Jennifer, Hecate, Macbeth, William McKinley, and Me, Elizabeth* (Konigsburg 2001) a delightful story in which Jennifer claims she is a witch and has the spells to prove it. Another book, on approximately a second-grade reading level, *George's Marvelous Medicine* (Dahl 1981), has George trying to mix up the perfect cure to Grandma's nastiness, and Grandma is always making up concoctions.

A minilesson would be taught on the writing of concoctions or crazy recipes that could be used for silly medicine or spells. Begin the minilesson by showing models of recipes. Explain that like a recipe, "concoction recipes" should be written so others can follow. Show students a model concoction such as:

Wart Grower

> 1 teaspoon baking soda
> 1 teaspoon vinegar
> 1 piece of brown crayon
> Put crayon on someone's hand. Mix vinegar and baking soda.
> Pour over crayon.

Together with the class, write another concoction, such as hair remover, measles maker, or pimple popper (sorry, but they'll love it). Now, they have been fully prepared to write a concoction at the writing center.

To give students more creative writing and a further challenge, a follow-up minilesson could be done on writing spells. Using spells from Konigsburg's book as examples, students could also write a spell to go with their concoction. Only positive or silly spells should be allowed, such as a spell that will make mothers dance for ten minutes or will cause a dog to chase its tail.

In contrast, some assigned writings for the center might need a series of minilessons to ensure optimal learning and accurate application of the task. Writing a comic strip at the writing center would take at least three minilessons. These could be taught to the whole class, although the students may be writing a comic book summary about the book they are reading in their guided reading groups. In this case the books chosen for each group should have lots of dialogue and action. The first minilesson would focus on writing dialogue from the book the students are reading. The second lesson's focus would be on the difference in design and text structure between thought balloons, speech balloons, and narrative text in the comic. The third minilesson should be on deciding how much of the incident being described should be included, and finally a fourth minilesson on how to set up the actual comic strip. As these minilessons are taught, students can begin their comic strip. After the first lesson on dialogue, students are ready to begin choosing and drafting dialogue they may include. As the other minilessons expand the learning, students will revise and edit using the new knowledge gained.

CHAPTER 11

Using Centers Effectively and with Accountability

"That's awesome!" Alicia exclaims as she notices her celery that has turned blue overnight. Now she asks what would happen if she split the celery part way up the stem, put one half in a cup with blue-colored water, the other half in red-colored water. Her question is, "Would the top turn purple?" Purple, she explains, is her favorite color. This sixth-grade mind is spinning faster than mine. I don't have a clue. Alicia's teacher, Ms. Todd, says next time she is at the science center she should write up the experiment and the hypothesis and try it out. Alicia, like me, wants to know sooner. Ms. Todd agrees that Alicia can begin this during her free time but must document the experiment. Alicia agrees and I observe a budding scientist begin her work.

Ms. Todd loves using centers in her classroom and is thrilled with this enthusiasm. She is confident that the center is well supplied. She knows Alicia will not cause problems if others are working at the center and in fact may increase the learning of others working with her.

Once you have made the decision that the pros outweigh the cons of using centers, it is time to get serious. Strong organization of all three types of centers—stationary, portable, and cruise—along with specified high expectations for completed tasks will result in effective use. On the other hand, loosey-goosey hurriedly thrown together centers will not get the needed results. Centers are learning tools and need to be kept organized, curriculum focused, user-friendly, and teacher-friendly. Teacher-friendly, in this instance, means that the students are responsible to have everything at the center ready for the next person's use when they are finished. The teacher's responsibility is to make sure the center is user-friendly and stocked with necessary materials.

Flowing with the Curriculum

Center ideas may stem directly from the curriculum or come from beyond the curriculum, giving student current materials and/or interesting topics for enrichment. Centers that stem from the curriculum can include activities that have previously been done with the class or new activities that reinforce and extend. When the center "flows with the curriculum," it is like a good friend. Familiar enough for the students to know something about it, it still offers some new areas to discover and learn. A center that flows with the curriculum follows or enriches what is taught in class. This might be themed on a topic being covered in class, repeating an activity that the class has done together, or making small changes to a task that had been completed previously and is being used to reinforce the information learned.

For instance, Mrs. Alver's plans flowed with the curriculum when her fifth-grade guided reading groups read creation tales that were on their instructional level. Mrs. Alvers taught a whole-class lesson, as she explained creation tales and what makes them unique. She then began meeting with the instructional-level groups and reinforced the components of creation tales as they read their respective books. Mrs. Alvers has plans to flow with the curriculum. She is going to set up the writing center with accordion books that students will use to make their own creation tale. Students will be using their own reading books as a model for this tale. Mrs. Alvers will offer a series of minilessons prior to assigning this center activity. She will model how to begin a creation tale, techniques in brainstorming the story line, and explain thoroughly her expectations of the finished product within the accordion book.

In another example, Mr. Taylor began his kindergarteners' week by reading the big book of *Ten, Nine, Eight* (Bang 1983). This book infers subtraction as it goes from ten clean toes to one little girl in bed. Mr. Taylor has prepared stapled books and each page has a large number going from ten to one. Students at the writing center are writing their own Ten, Nine, Eight books. The only "rule" Mr. Taylor has given them is that the one has to be them doing something, just like the little girl in bed. They may end up at school, having lunch, or going somewhere. The students need to draw a picture including the objects, making sure the number of objects corresponds with the number on the page, and write a phrase about the picture. Mr. Taylor's students are engaged at the center. They are writing a fact-based or completely imaginary book about themselves; they brainstorm and "draft" when talking to other students at the center; and they understand the expectations. Mr. Taylor, with minimal work, has managed to create a center activity that flows with the curriculum. He figures if the students do a page or two a day, this activity should last about two weeks.

Ms. Nunez's first-grade class is working on onsets and rimes. She has purchased some matching cards in which the onset can be put together with the rimes—for example, the onset *m* can be put together with the rime *op* to make *mop*. The class has been working with the rimes *op, at, it,* and *an* as these rimes have been the focus of books read in class. Ms. Nunez has used the matching cards in small groups and now feels the students are ready to do this independently. She is going to put the onset/rime game at the word study center. Students will be instructed to match the cards and to write two words from each of the rimes, which will be handed in as their center work. This word study center flows with the curriculum as it is reinforcing phonological skills being taught in class.

Mr. Robert's fifth-grade class had been studying China. The students are interested in the Chinese calendar. They have decided to create a mural of one the characters for the hallway. Mr. Robert's class thinks other students will be interested in what year they were born in because it is a year of one of the following animals: rat, ox, tiger, rabbit, dragon, snake, horse, sheep, monkey, rooster, dog, and pig. They are drawing the animals, writing down the years that would include all the students at their school, and the personality that goes with the year. Students work on this during their center time. When the showcase calendar is done, Mr. Roberts will have the students write a personal response to the calendar. He wants the students to state what year they were born and the corresponding animal. He then wants the students to say whether they feel they do or do not have the characteristics given with the animal. For instance, if they were born in the year of the tiger, do they consider themselves brave and loyal like the tiger? Mr. Roberts then wants students to support this by writing their actions that make them like or unlike the animal of their Chinese birth year.

Having the students self-analyze their own personality/character is very important because Mr. Roberts has bigger plans. This Chinese calendar center activity will flow with the curriculum as Mr. Roberts is going to start focusing on character development with the next guided reading books. He has reading groups on fourth-, fifth- and sixth-grade levels. Mr. Roberts has chosen books that include strong character development to use with each group. His next center activity will have students following the main character's development throughout the chapters. When the leveled reading groups have finished their books and analyzed the character, Mr. Roberts will go back to the Chinese calendar and have students match book characters to what month they might have been born when using the character traits on the Chinese calendar.

Getting Centers to Work

How Do You Start?

There are two recommended ways to begin using centers. One school of thought from experienced center users is to start small. Begin with three or four easy to establish and maintain centers, such as reading, writing, word study, and listening centers. Only allow a certain number at each center. Initially, have the rest of the class do independent reading at their seats while other students do center time. Once all students have learned how to use the centers, start meeting with the leveled reading groups as children do their centers. In contrast, some center users think that classrooms should have a minimum of seven centers, that the number of students should be limited at each center, and that the larger number of centers avoids crowds.

Making centers work effectively becomes routine once you have the structure in place. The word *routine* is the key. We all know that when routines are maintained, the students are more likely to follow them and, in reality, routine is easier for us too! It is imperative that students understand what they are doing when they go to a center. As explained in the previous chapter on minilessons, the topic needs to be taught, the center needs to be introduced, and the procedures explained. If you begin your centers with activities from minilessons that have been used with the whole class or reading groups, your explanations will be less time-consuming and students will feel more confident when doing the work.

Who Goes Where? When?

There are a number of ways to decide who should go to which center or to limit the number of students at each center. Teachers need to do what is comfortable for their teaching styles. Some of us love structure and feel more comfortable assigning students to a particular center daily. Others love to give children choices and prefer to allow students to choose to which center they want to go.

The following ideas can be used to assign centers.

■ Centers can be numbered, and students can be given a paper weekly that tells them which center to go to daily.

■ A center board can be used, and the children's name can be placed under the center they are to go to that day.

■ Center time can be structured weekly, so students know which one or two centers they are to go to daily, and this remains the same on any given Monday, Tuesday, and so on.

- Center cards can be placed at the children's seats daily. If a student finds the listening center picture or icon at his desk or table when he comes into school, he knows which center he has for the day. (This method helps with individualization, because if Samantha was hesitant working with the CVCe (Consonant, Vowel, Consonant, silent e) pattern yesterday, you can send her to the phonics center today to work on this skill.)

- A rotating wheel can be used in a way that the wheel is moved one center ahead each day to allow students to rotate through all the centers.

- Clothespin markers can be used. Clothespins with each child's name are clipped to the center picture or icon they are to go to that day. This has the same result as putting the icon on the child's desk or table. In this case some students may have to come up to check which center they are to go to; in the other scenario the picture or icons are often lost.

For those who prefer student choice, the following center systems have been used.

- Simply free choice. Students know they can go to any center they want. In this case the classroom needs to have at least seven centers, and the teacher needs to have activities at each center that would encourage student choice.

- Using clothespins with children's names, the students clip the clothespin on the center of their choice. The number of students can easily be limited. For instance, students can be told that only four students may be at the listening center. On the icon of that center, there should be four tally marks. Students should clip their clothespin on a tally mark. When all tally marks have been covered (four clothespins are up), the center is full for this session and no one else can join them.

- With younger children, color code the centers. Have necklaces of the same color available. So, if the listening center can have four students, it would be colored coded blue, and only four blue necklaces would be available. If only two students are allowed at the computer center, the computer center would be green, and only two green necklaces would be available. Because the little students have no qualms about wearing the necklaces, it's easy to see that they are in the correct place! For older students use the "slap on" bracelets that were in vogue a few years back but can be found at discount stores today. Buy the bracelets of various designs, hang one on the center, and use the matching bracelets for the students.

■ Limit the chairs. Make a rule that all children must sit at the centers and that if there are no empty chairs, they must find a different center. For centers where chairs may not be used, chair pictures can be available. For instance, at the reading center, in which students are allowed to sit in the big plastic pool for a "cool read," chair pictures can be hung on hooks, and students put a chair picture in a bag or basket to symbolize their space at the center.

Can You Organize Accountability?

Effective use of centers includes accountability. Confucius Nancy says that at centers "He who can, will waste time"—unfortunately, also some of the teacher's time and that of other students. Accountability must be built into the center and include three aspects. First, that the center tasks have been designed to teach or reinforce a skill, strategy, or content. Second, that there is plan to ensure students have completed center tasks. Third, the center products, or the processes of learning at the center, have been done successfully. The first aspect, designing centers to teach or reinforce a skill, strategy, or content is focused on during center planning time. For kindergartners, putting a puzzle together of a mammal would be developmentally appropriate for both fine motor skills and content. This same idea at a third-grade puzzle center is most likely not appropriate. On the other hand, if the puzzle in this third-grade class was one of the United States and students had to make the puzzle, pick a Midwestern state, and write the state and the states that border it, the center has a justifiable content focus.

The second aspect, a plan to ensure students have completed center tasks, needs to be one of the foci of the teacher's center management system. The center activity does not have to be designed to be completed in one day, but there needs to be a checkpoint to ensure students are working responsibly. For some centers, that may mean a quick check by the teacher. For kindergarten and beginning first graders a minute walk around the room between reading groups can gather a mountain of insight and information for the teacher and get some students back on track to learning. The teacher can check quickly to see if the task was done correctly and completely. Also, a partner check can be used. Partner students with someone who has done the center, and have them check in on the work being done.

Once students are capable of being responsible for the completion of their own work, they need to be held accountable! If the center is activity based and does not necessarily result in a written or created product, a summary sheet can be used. For example, at the phonics center students are working with onsets and rimes. The rime is *ot* and the onset letters are *c, d, g, h, l, n, p,* and *t.* There are three activities: one is a wheel, in which the onset letters turn, making a new word with the *ot* rime, the second is a pocket chart where students put the letters in front of the rime to form the word; the third activity has students using magnet letters to make the *ot* words. The summary sheet has the student tracing three of the magnetic letter words and drawing a visual describing the word in some way. It is the summary sheet that must be handed in for student accountability.

Sometimes there is a center activity in which this type of summary sheet doesn't make sense. Let's say the class is reading *Bud, Not Buddy* (Curtis 1999) and are studying the depression. At one of the centers students are making a mural depicting scenes from the depression era. The center has a selection of wonderful picture books, encyclopedias, and nonfiction material on the depression. Students are to read and select something from the reading to represent on the mural. The summary sheet (Appendix 11–1) can be used. This generic sheet asks students to explain what is being done at the center, what they did that day, and why they chose to do this.

The third aspect of successful centers, that of the center products or the processes of learning at the center being done successfully, refers to the teacher's accountability to monitor student progress. We, of course, not only have the students doing the work but we have to make sure they are doing it correctly. Centers must include something that verifies students' understanding of the center work and be monitored for tasks completed.

Keeping Track

Once, when visiting a classroom, a student teacher of mine was keeping track of student's homework assignments, and what each student had due. She had a large poster board with each student's name. The assignments were numbered, and ones that had been turned in were checked off. This was a daily ritual for the last ten minutes of class. What a waste. One hundred eighty days times ten comes to eighteen hundred minutes or thirty hours of class time. There is not much exaggeration here. Even if this homework check were done every other school day, it would be fifteen hours of classroom instruction time lost. Obviously we have to do better. The summary sheet collection has to be organized and quickly accounted for or checked when students are otherwise engaged.

Students' work can be collected in a variety of ways. Some ideas that have been proven useful:

- In boxes: Students can be told to put all the center papers in a specified in box, or the teacher may prefer to have an in box at every center.

- Checklists: The teacher, a parent, or responsible students can use a checklist with names to make sure all students who were to hand in a summary sheet did so.

- Folders: Some teachers prefer to give students the inexpensive colored folders with pockets. Students put their center work in their folders and the teacher collects the folders at his convenience.

- Shoe storage boxes: Using two of the cardboard shoe storage containers, students put their papers in the small "cubby" with their name.

- Shoe storage hangers: Hanging shoe storage comes with room for twelve pairs of shoes. If a class has twenty-four or fewer students, two of these hangers can be hung low in the classroom, with a student's name on each pocket. Students put their daily center work in their pocket.

- Clothesline: This is my personal favorite because students' completed work can be so easily seen. A clothesline is hung under the chalkboard or white board, down the whole length of the room. Clothespins with students' names are put on the clothesline. As students finish their center time, they hang their completed work or summary sheet on the clothesline, using their clothespin. When checking for completed work, a teacher can instantly tell whether a student has been responsible in handing in her finished paper or summary sheet. When the finished project is a bulky item, the student takes from a basket an index card with a generic icon symbolizing a completed project and hangs that with his clothespin.

Sometimes centers have projects that are to be completed over a number of visits. If children are not keeping their own folders, or even if they are, it might be best to use a Scarlett O'Hara box. This is a box at the center in which students place their incomplete work to be finished "tomorrow." Eventually, the project will be done and will have to be submitted to the teacher in the expected fashion.

The management of centers is often the key to whether or not teachers enjoy using them. If items are disorganized and lost or students are unruly and irresponsible, centers quickly wear thin. Using strategies and techniques given in this chapter ensures that each center will be the motivating and engaged learning activity it should be.

Summary Sheet

Name_____

What is this center about?

What did you do at this center today?

Why did you decide to do this?

©2007 by Nancy L. Witherell from *The Guided Reading Classroom*. Portsmouth, NH: Heinemann.

CHAPTER 12

More Ideas for Stationary, Portable, and Mobile Centers

Let's step into the classrooms of Ms. Daley and Mrs. Susi, fourth-grade team teachers. They have twelve centers between the two rooms that are connected by an adjoining door. Students use centers in both rooms and the teachers have agreed to maintain the centers in their own classrooms. Most centers have two students at them, one from Ms. Daley's class and the other from Mrs. Susi's. Because the teachers team for reading, some of the students in Ms. Daley's class have Mrs. Susi for reading and vice versa. The teachers feel they can more accurately reach the students' reading levels with this teaching arrangement. It is definitely a student-centered classroom.

Most centers are stationary. The rooms are big, and the teachers are creative. One center uses magnets to keep the pieces on the side of the file cabinet, so students can match compound words then write a list to hand in. Another center is a basket with large-print items from newspapers. This portable center stems off a story in the fourth-grade anthology in which a boy receives an anonymous note in large cutout newspaper print. Students bring this to their worktable and write and design "acceptable" anonymous letters. They can be given to anyone in the students' lives—a custodian, a grandmother, or someone else in the room—once a teacher has checked the letter. Two sample newspaper print letters are taped above the basket, one Ms. Daley made as a model and the other made by Sarah, a student in the class. The night after Ms. Daley explained the newspaper print letters, Sarah was so enthusiastic about the idea she went home and wrote a note to Ms. Daley.

Ms. Daley and Mrs. Susi change a few of the centers about every three weeks. The ideas stem off the curriculum and their professional reading. Over the years they have learned to repeat centers or pieces of centers at appropriate times. They have lives, and can only put so much time into center creation. They have learned to get more with less.

Getting More with Less: Creating and Maintaining Centers

As described in Chapter 11 there are basically three types of centers: stationary (permanently set up in the room), portable (materials are in a container and brought to a work area or desk), and cruise (students move around the room and complete designated activities with material in the room). The focus of this chapter is twofold: to share a variety of topics for center use and to offer concrete ideas for use with some of the topics. Staying close to the theme of doing more with less, the ideas given can be easily connected with curriculum. Many of the activities can be used with guided reading groups or with the whole class. The stationary centers are designed to have minimal upkeep; the others may require more work.

When choosing centers and the learning activities, there are two considerations: the developmental level of the students and the amount of teacher time needed to prepare and maintain the center. We know developmental appropriateness goes beyond grade level. Teachers often say, "Well, my class last year could have done this, but this year's class will not be able to manage." Or, "This class just seems to have it all together, I can do so much more with them." If centers are designed with open-ended responses, they can be used with multiple-level learners. This also holds true when centers contain different levels of activities. Some years, activities must be simplified or made more complex. This is also why centers have two different storage places. One is where they are kept for children's use; the other is where the materials are kept when not in use because sometimes when a center is not developmentally appropriate for a particular class the materials are stored for a whole year!

When it comes to the preparation time involved, teachers need to decide what they can handle. If you are going home to two children, cooking dinner, giving baths, organizing and helping with homework, reading to the kids nightly—centers should be kept simple! On the other hand, prior to having my three boys, I enjoyed making materials for centers and creating new and challenging activities. Let's emphasize the word *prior*: when kids arrive, life changes!

When reading through the ideas offered in this chapter, think about your own situation. How much time can you invest? Some centers, such as the computer center, take minimal time, without compromising the learning. Other centers, like the word study center, may take a great deal of time to prepare. Making activities where students match a word to its meaning or offering a cloze activity using manipulatives takes time to create, especially if you are flowing through the curriculum, therefore using words from the current guided reading books or anthology. A cloze activity has students using context to fill in the blank, for instance, "The man ____ the car." The students would then have to pick from the choices of *drive* or *drove*. The sentence would be written on an index card, and then students would be given words to place in the blank. For accountability, the teacher can check the work at the center's completion or number the sentences and have students write answers only on a paper to be checked later.

Purchasing manipulatives saves time. There are a number of catalogs that list a huge variety of resources. Many are quite good and follow the mainstream curriculum. Also, most basal programs offer activities for phonics or picture cards for vocabulary growth. These can be easily adapted for center use and because they are often used in guided reading groups, they reinforce the curriculum. Internet sites with free ideas or resources for sale can be found by searching under "center manipulatives for reading and language arts." Authors such as Jan Brett and Patricia Polacco have on their websites downloadable material and ideas to use with their books.

This chapter discusses center ideas for the three types of centers. Think about what centers will work in your room. Read the pieces that interest you. If the bodies in your classroom are too big and the physical place too small for stationary centers, skip that portion (unless you want the ideas) and delve right into portable centers. If you can't stand students roaming the room, skip the cruise center section. It is not the type of center that is important; the materials, objectives, and curriculum are top priority.

Stationary Learning Centers: Space to Work

Stationary centers can cover a variety of topics and be arranged in multiple ways. Each stationary center can have a number of activities, as long as there is space. When the area is too crowded and items begin to fall on the floor, things start to get complicated and uncomfortable. The centers should offer a variety of activities. When renewing centers, some of the activities can stay while some are exchanged with new ones. Some teachers store the extra center activities in ziplock bags in a plastic container under the center table.

The following centers are recommended for use with guided reading (Fountas and Pinnell 1996, Owocki 2005, Diller 2003).

Browsing Boxes, Baskets, or Independent Reading

This center offers free reading materials. Books are placed in boxes or baskets and leveled so children will know which basket to choose from. This center is extremely simple. For accountability you can simply have students write their name on an index card and the number of books they read during browsing time. This center should be just plain comfortable and fun. Teachers are very creative with this area and use the following items: futons, big pillows, rugs, tents, rocking chairs, beanbags, small swimming pools, benches, and as mentioned before, even bathtubs!

Buddy Reading

This center fosters buddy reading, either assigned or free choice. Students can reread to each other with expression and work on fluency techniques. Students should know how to select books at their just right level, or the books can be leveled in baskets. If the buddies are on different levels, they can read books at their own levels to each other or support each other in these books.

Letter Centers: Working with the Alphabet

For very young children the letter center can reinforce both letter recognition and letter sound. Students can work with clay or finger paint; use markers to make huge letters on old newspapers; work with magnetic letters or plastic letters, practicing letters on white boards; use letters on felt boards, matching letters to pictures of words that begin with the sound; and so forth. The ideas are endless and can go from phonemic awareness activities to reinforcing phonics by working with phonics generalizations.

Word Study Center

This center is equipped with all things literacy. Activities and materials can include: pictures and words to increase vocabulary, word games, word matches, white boards to practice words, picture dictionaries, children's dictionaries, a thesaurus, interesting books that give word history (etymology), posters explaining word endings, lists of affixes, and manipulatives used in the reading groups. Students can be given choices of what to do such as: make their own dictionary, add to a class thesaurus, make vocabulary cards, complete activities that have students working with word endings or affixes. Teachers may direct a certain activity at the center or let the students have free choice. Students would be accountable by completing a summary sheet explaining what they did.

Listening Centers

The listening center can highlight the books being read by the guided reading groups or contain a choice of books that students will enjoy. A prelistening activity, writing or drawing a prediction of what the book will be about, and a postlistening activity, writing or drawing what happened in the book (see Appendix 12–1), can be used. Having students make connections or write and describe the funniest, most surprising, or most poignant portion of the story can also be done to vary activities at the center.

Arts and Crafts Center

The art center should focus on literacy and text comprehension. Teachers can direct students to respond to a book read in class, their guided reading book, or books from the listening center. The art center should contain a variety of art materials: markers, chalk, clay, paper, old magazines, small boxes for dioramas, fabric, ribbon and any material pertinent to books being read. It is important to focus students on the literacy event as they create an art project. Some focus ideas: Students can make a three-dimensional map of the setting of a book and label the areas, a scene depicting emotions in the story can be drawn accompanied by a sentence explaining it, characters can be depicted through a collage of magazine pictures, or clay can be molded to portray the mood of a book chapter.

Writing Center

The activities at the writing center can be required or a list of choices can be posted. Some ideas students can choose from include the following.

- Write a letter to a character.

- Write a four-part summary of the book (on accordion folded paper).

- Write a prequel or a sequel.

- Write an advertisement for the book.

- Write a newspaper article of an important event.

- Choose a character you would like to spend a day with and explain why.

- Explain how the story problem could have been solved differently.

- Write a summary of the book with drawing to illustrate it.

- Write an advertisement for the book.

- Write the weather report that would have been given in the book.

- Write a book review to encourage or discourage students from reading the book.

- Write a poem that describes the character.

- Explain what you would have done in the character's place.

- Illustrate story with pictures and captions.

- Write a letter to the author.

Students can also work on ongoing projects such as writing a book, readers' theatre, or a play.

The writing center should be supplied with all types of writing materials. Some of the best supplies for writing centers come from the quarter or dollar boxes at local yard sales: opened or unopened boxes of stationery and cards, writing journals and notebooks, interesting paper and wrapping paper (for book covers). One idea is to make small books using wrapping paper as the cover. Students write a story that uses the wrapping paper pictures as the subject of the book: for instance, sports paper would house writings about sports, as papers with pandas, beach pails, or whatever theme would lead to writings about that theme. The writing center should also include a list of frequently misspelled words, a dictionary, and a thesaurus.

Theater or Drama Center

This center encourages students to write plays and to act out stories. They can do a readers' theater or retell a book by giving a play. The number of characters in the book the students are reading can dictate the number of students at this center, or students can be given the liberty to change the story so the number of students at the center match the number of characters in the story.

Generic costumes and cloth should be available. The costumes available for use should be changed with the books being read in the classroom. For instance, if the book is about pioneers, bonnets would be appropriate, but they would not be needed for a Junie B. Jones book. These, by the way, are also great yard sale finds. If the center uses hats, which are so much fun, require students to put a paper "cover" on their heads first.

Overhead Projector

An overhead projector can be used for a multitude of purposes: phonics reinforcement, word usage, cloze procedures, project displays, and so forth. For students, this is a motivating tool; they can do their work and make shadows too. The projector must be placed low and be secured. It is very easy to make or have made black-and-white and colored transparencies with which a variety of activities can be done. Students can read poems together or practice fluency by rereading a portion of the book. They can reread the morning messages or practice handwriting (Diller 2003). Students can be told to circle words that begin like *ham* or words that rhyme. They can use magnetic letters to form words on the screen (Fountas and Pinnell 1996, Diller 2003). Students can also cut out small character shapes and write and perform a shadow play summarizing a story they have read.

Retelling Center

The focus of this center is to support students as they practice retelling stories they have read. The most dependent students can use a roll chart to retell the story. The roll chart has every picture in the book glued on it, and students "walk the line" as they retell the story using the sequentially ordered pictures to help them. A variation of this is storyboards, which depict the action and sequence of a story, and students can follow the story line to retell the story. These are usually made on poster board and have a line with arrows to aid students in the proper sequence. A higher level of difficulty than using the storyboard is using puppets. Puppets depicting the characters and setting can be available to aid in the retelling. The puppets help students recall the characters and some of the plot, but students must remember the sequence on their own. Finally, a more challenging activity has students making their own puppets or props. This requires students to recall the characters and the plot.

Pocket Chart

Pocket charts come in all shapes and sizes. I made my own pocket chart by putting colored plastic over plywood and stapling on clear plastic for the pockets. The board stiffens the chart and makes it easier to manipulate the word, number, and letter cards that are placed in them. Activities with pocket charts are endless. Students can use pocket charts to

- sequence

- make words, sort words, or rhyme words

- put a sentence or poem in order

- match color with color words

- match number to number words

- match capital letters to lowercase letters

- put days and months in order

- follow phonics patterns and experiment with end marks

Older students can:

- group synonyms

- work with derivatives, affixes, tenses

- do word sorts with content area vocabulary

- sequence directions or a story

- match capitals to the right state

- put words in alphabetical order, to the fourth letter if needed

Read Aloud Center

The main purpose of a read-aloud center is to help students gain fluency, but it differs from buddy reading because the reading material is different. The reading material consists of texts that are written or lend themselves to be read aloud with exaggerated expression. Because students will be working together reading aloud, this center should be on the far side of the room from the students' work area. This center would include puppets and some puppet shows to read, readers' theatre materials, radio scripts, passages for reading, and a tape recorder. Students can tape themselves reading and listen to the tape, having been told to pay attention to their tone and expression. Once students have practiced you can have them read to other students or send the listening tape off to a nursing home for the enjoyment of the elderly (Prescott-Griffin and Witherell 2004). You may choose to alternate use of the buddy reading center with this center.

Other Ideas

Some other ideas for stationary center topics include: cooking, science, math (from Fountas and Pinnell 1996), computer, word game, poetry, flannel board, magnetic board, create a book, season/holiday focus, and skills centers. These centers can be designed to focus on the curriculum and include all types of literacy activities.

Portable Learning Centers: Activities in a Box

Portable centers can be a miniscale of stationary centers or they can have a narrower focus. Each container needs to be a complete center with all components, including any paperwork that must be done. Students need to know where in the room they are allowed to do the portable center work and the number of students allowed. A form (Appendix 12–2) can be taped to the top outside of the shoeboxes and pizza boxes or laminated and attached to a wicker basket. This form gives the name of the center, the number of students who may use it, and where it is to be returned. For very young children, put an icon on the box that represents the center and the same icon on the shelf where it is to be returned. Draw a stick person for the number of students that can use the portable center at one time.

Whether they are put in a shoebox, pizza box, or a wicker basket, there should be a list of the components. The number of items allows students to quickly count to ensure all items are there. In the case of a set of cards, they can be placed in a ziplock sandwich bag and the bag will count as one item to simplify things. Students will have to be given an explanation of the components and the rules of "packing up" and returning the portable centers.

Pizza boxes are great for including small game boards. The game board can be the size of a pizza box, or double if folded. Manila folders will fit into a large pizza box; they make sturdy enough game boards and come in a variety of bright colors. The dice or spinner and all game pieces should fit inside the pizza box. In addition, a nonending game works well. In a game without end, there is no finish on the game board. The student who is ahead at the end of center time is the winner.

A whole book could be written on portable center ideas. There are a great number of books that have phonics activities and word study ideas. Portable center activities can be purchased and remain in the box that they come in (simply tape the center information form on top). There are commercially boxed products that teach onset and rime, rhyming skills, alphabetical order, and VCe (Vowel, Consonant, silent e) pattern, to name a few.

Many of the phonics and manipulative activities should also be used with guided reading or skills groups.

To help students succeed at these centers, the learning activities can be numbered from easiest to hardest, and the teacher should tell the student which number to begin with. Most of the following ideas offer activities in a numbered sequence purposefully set up so students will go from the easiest to the hardest. For some classrooms using two of the activities may be appropriate. These ideas are offered for teachers to expand upon and improve. Some portable center ideas follow.

Listening Center

Use a small CD or tape player that runs on batteries. Have the book and a pre/postreading sheet in the box (for accountability; see Appendix 12–1). This center would be limited to one person, but more boxes could be set up the same way with the same or different books. Teachers often tell me they don't have room for listening centers or they don't have the headsets needed. The cost for an individual listener in this case is minimal. Old tape recorders, now outdated by CD players, are cheap yard sale finds and headsets can be found at the dollar store—they sell for two dollars on an airplane!

Phonics Center

The container (box or basket) should have multiple activities on the same skill. For instance, if students were learning the short *a* sound, the center could have the following three activities.

1. Matching game: cards to match word with picture, all words with short *a* sounds.

2. "Ah Apple" activity: a sandwich bag with an apple taped on top, pictures of twelve different items (hat, sun, pan, and so forth). Students are to put the picture of the words with the short *a* sound in the "Ah Apple" bag.

3. Pictures of short rhyming words: students are to sort the pictures of the words on a mat that spells the ending sound. For instance, three ending sounds: *at*, *ap*, and *ag*. Pictures of the following will be placed in the appropriate area: hat, mat, cat, rat, cap, lap, map, bag, hag, rag, tag, wag.

For accountability, the teacher can have students save one of the finished activities to be checked, or students can write five of the short *a* words and draw pictures to show what the words mean.

Contraction Action

This box would focus on contractions and could include the following three activities.

1. Match the contraction with the two words it is derived from.

2. Use a dry erase marker to write the missing letter from the contraction to separate the two words they are derived from.

3. Use a board game where the student rolls dice and picks a card. If he can give the two words that form the contraction, he may move forward the number on the dice. (Cards will have to lie contraction side up; students can check the answers that are written on the back of the card.)

Ocean of Opposites (Antonyms)

Using an ocean theme, this portable center would have three activities with opposites. This center would be cute in a plastic fish bowl.

1. Two clam shells that would be put together by matching the opposite words such as *up/down* and *cold/hot*.

2. Small fishing pole with a magnet and eight fish to catch (with paper clips at the mouth) and eight drawn fishbowls. The fishbowls and fish would have matching opposite words written on them. Students would "catch" a fish with the word *happy* on it and place the fish on the fishbowl with the word *sad* written on it.

3. Four sets of double hooks (plastic ones or drawn), and eight worms. Each hook will have an opposite that matches two of the worms. Students match worms to correct hook. The words could be: *light* to match *dark* and *dim*, *ugly* to match *pretty* and *beautiful*, *mean* to match *nice* and *kind*, and then *chubby* to match *skinny* and *thin*.

Synonym Soup

This center helps students match words that mean the same and it would be cute in a big plastic bowl for a container. Three possible activities follow.

1. Match words that mean the same by matching a spoon with a word on it to a bowl. These can be drawn pictures or words written on plastic spoons and paper bowls.

2. Using a wooden spoon, students spoon one word out of a bowl (could be a large bowl or paper bowl). Then, they spoon out a second word. The challenge is to get the matching word out of the bowl within two tries.

3. Using alphabet noodles students glue spelling words and matching synonyms onto construction paper.

More Than One: *s, es* (or *i*)?

This portable center focuses on when to add the ending *s* or *es* to pluralize words. Or should I say the foci are *s* and *es* endings? The *i* pluralization rule should be added to challenge capable students. Depending on the students' knowledge of plurals, it might be best that irregular plurals (*mouse* to *mice*) not be included but can be used at a subsequent center. The rule, changing the *y* to *i* and adding *es*, but not if a vowel comes before the *y*, may also be for a different center at a later time. Three activities follow that would go well in this center in which students are practicing adding *s* or *es*.

1. Matching: Have pictures showing one item and then a picture showing more than one of the same items. Have two cards, one with the singular and one with the plural. The students are to match all four cards into the same set (see Figure 12–1).

2. Categorizing: Students are to categorize words by putting them in a cup labeled *s* or a cup labeled *es*; for example, *pail* would go into the *s* cup, *church* would go into the *es* cup. (The answer should be written in small print on the back of the word card.) When the two piles are separated, the student can self-check to see if they are right.

3. Using the same cards from activity 2, students pick five of the words and use them in sentences (this is to be handed in).

Vocabulary-Building Activities

Vocabulary should come from words being used in the current curriculum to reinforce word meaning. Shoebox centers can house a myriad of vocabulary activities. Three ideas follow.

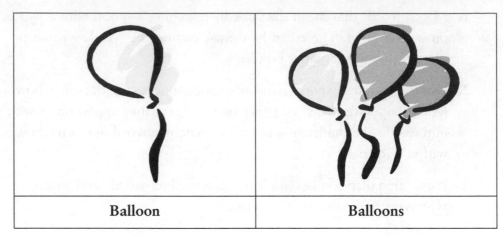

| Balloon | Balloons |

Figure 12–1. *Picture/Word Match Plurals*

1. Students can match words to their meaning.

2. Students can make their own vocabulary cards, put the meaning in their own words, and draw an illustration.

3. The cards for activity 1 can be used in a Concentration game. Some other ideas for vocabulary centers: context activities, word sorts, using a dictionary, or making a dictionary of personal words.

Story Follow-up Activities

Story follow-up activities for a portable center should stem from books or stories being read by or to the whole class. Although it is more interesting if the activities are different from response tasks that are assigned with the guided reading books, most any type of response can be used. Some more unusual learning center activities might be:

1. straw puppets to do a retelling

2. using three mini–white boards to show the beginning, middle, and end of the story

3. clay or paint to depict an important part of the story, with this description written on an index card

Cruise Centers: No Place Like Roam

Cruise centers allow at least one more center in the room, without much preparation and with no other space being utilized. The cruise center reinforces curriculum in a fun and inviting way. This is one time when you are not saying to a student, "Sit down!" Students learn, move, and enjoy.

Accountability can be more difficult with cruise centers unless you are using an activity that requires a particular product. Otherwise a summary should be required, where the student explains what he did and how it helped his learning. Management can also be more difficult, but if students understand they do not disturb others at work, this problem is lessened. Children love the freedom of cruise centers. It gives them time to legally explore their classroom and to be attentive to what is there.

Read the Room

This mobile center is well defined by Fountas and Pinnell (1996). Students walk around the room and read material posted on walls or hanging in various places. The students carry a pointer and read charts, poems, and other written material. They usually work with partners and help each other out. This center enables students to practice material already read and reinforces vocabulary.

Moving Math Focus

In the quest to reinforce math concepts and writing across the curriculum, students can be given tasks to support what they are learning in math. For instance, students can be asked to find objects in the room that are a certain length, say two inches. They must write a sentence or complete a sentence that says, "An object in my room that measures two inches is _____. I measured this by _____. Another object that measures two inches is _____. I measured this by _____." A similar set-up can be done with weight or comparing weights. Some other math center ideas that incorporate reading and writing follow.

Finding math sets: Students can also be told to look for sets of objects and write the description of these sets in a sentence. Answers will vary, but some examples: "I found a set of two pencils, one was yellow and one was red." "I found a set of four pictures. They are on the bulletin board with New England States."

Reinforcing time: Using a stopwatch students would walk for predetermined intervals of time. The task sheet may say, "Walk around the room and stop in fifteen seconds. Write and describe what you are near now." This can be done for five seconds, ten seconds, and so forth.

Fractions: For fractions students will identify subsets of sets. See Appendix

12–3 for a generic sample that can be used when developmentally appropriate. A basket of books must be set up for this activity. For older students, a similar activity can be designed to reinforce ratio.

Mapping It Out

Using a compass and a predetermined set of directions, have students roam the room and find the "final destination." Written directions can include text like "Walk north three steps, turn east for six. Describe where you are." Continue with three more similar sets of directions. If they end up approximately where they should, you know they understand the function of a compass. Students can also be asked to draw and label a map of their "travels."

Rhyme Time

Give students a list of words. They must roam the room to find objects that rhyme with the words on the list. Students must write down the name of the rhyming object and where it was found. Some ideas: *cook (book, hook), darker (marker), kite (light, white), more (floor, door), bear (chair, air, D.A.R.E., hair, pair),* and *fox (box).*

Context Clues

Students can walk around the room and fill in the cloze activity by using their understanding of the context to fill in the blank. Some examples follow.

> I went to the _____ because my pencil was dull.
> The teacher sat at her _____ to read the story.
> I looked at the _____ to see what center to do.

Riddles

Riddles can be written in a clear or obtuse manner depending on appropriateness. First and second graders should be able to do the clear riddles, older students the obtuse. Some examples that pair the clear with obtuse follow.

> (Clear)   You read me to tell time. _____
> (Obtuse)   You can be late if you don't pay attention to me. _____
> (Clear)   You walk through me to get into the hall. _____
> (Obtuse)   If you stand under me you are neither in nor out. _____

Analogies

Students roam the room to find the objects that complete an analogy. Some examples follow:

Words are to books as numbers are to _____. (clocks)

Legs are to desks as walls are to the _____. (ceiling)

Lunch is to lunchbox as books are to _____. (shelves)

Broom is to floor as an eraser is to the _____. (chalk or white board)

Treasure Hunt

Although this cruise center takes more effort, the students' fun makes the small amount of extra work worthwhile. Treasure hunt has long been a children's game, in which hidden clues give a hint to find the next clue. After finding all the clues, the final destination brings students to a treasure. Clues may rhyme or not. For a literacy center, there should be at least six clues the students have to read and figure out. The first clue could be in an envelope in a basket. It may read, "If you want to see rain or snow, over to me you would go." Then the second clue would be taped to the window. The second clue may read, "When I ring, let me be . . . only the teacher speaks to me." So, the second clue would be on the class phone, which would house the third clue. Students follow the series of clues until they reach a spot that houses a small treasure. This final destination may end with the rhyme, "Here's your treasure, now you're done. I hope that you had lots of fun!" and is signed by the teacher.

In Conclusion

The number of center ideas in this chapter is minuscule compared to what can be done. The ideas shared here should be used and expanded upon. In most cases, the closer a teacher can get a center to flow with the curriculum, the less difficult and time-consuming the teacher preparation is, and the reinforcement aids in student recall of information. Centers bring vibrancy and energy into classrooms. They are most certainly worth a try!

Listening Center

Name _____

Name of book _____

Author _____

Look at the cover of the book and the pictures inside. What do you think will happen?

What happened?

©2007 by Nancy L. Witherell from *The Guided Reading Classroom*. Portsmouth, NH: Heinemann.

Center Name _____

_____ can use this center.

Place center back _____

❧ Remember to check the center inventory when done!

Center Name _____

_____ can use this center.

Place center back _____

❧ Remember to check the center inventory when done!

Center Name _____

_____ can use this center.

Place center back _____

❧ Remember to check the center inventory when done!

Look at the calendar in your classroom. How many days have gone by this month? _____

Write this in fraction form. _____

Explain how you figured this out:

Count the number of desks or tables in your classroom where children sit. _____ How many are empty?

_____ What fraction of tables or desks are empty? _____

Explain how you figured this out:

Choose a basket of books. Count the total number of books in the basket. _____ Count the number of

books that have the word *the* in the title. _____ What fraction of the books have the word *the* in the title?

_____

Explain how you figured this out:

Count the number of students in the classroom. _____ Count the number of students now reading a

book or magazine. _____ What fraction of all students are reading a book? _____

Explain how you figured this out:

CHAPTER 13

How It Works

Are you ready for this? Of course! You know how to organize and manage. The time put into managing guided reading programs is well worth the benefits: students who are reading on their instructional levels and who are continually growing as readers as assessment is guiding their instruction. The dilemma for most teachers is how to do this well, how to manage all facets of guided reading at the same time, and what to do if things are going wrong. Take it slow, start with comfortable pieces and add on, and . . . hang on. Guided reading is a series of routines. Find the routines that fit best with your teaching style.

This chapter is the "Dear Abby" of guided reading, except here it is "Dear Nancy." Having aided teachers in the bumps of guided reading, the following scenarios come from questions that have been asked. Each problem given has multiple options to help in bringing a solution. Ultimately the teacher needs to decide what might work for her.

Excerpts from the Guided Reading Gazette

Dear Nancy,

Woe is me! I am beside myself. My school district is really pushing us into guided reading. They have had experts come in the afternoon for professional development and we had two full day trainings while the district hired subs. I am reluctant to start. I'm afraid I will fail. My principal has offered me time to visit other schools. But, gee, my kids get enough interruptions in their learning and I just had the two professional days where they had a sub. I don't want to leave them for another day. I just don't have the guts to get started with this stuff. What should I do?

Sincerely,

Chickenhearted in Toronto

Dear Chickenhearted,

It is okay to be nervous about starting guided reading. Anything new is nerve-wracking, change is scary, and you will be making big changes in your classroom. Focus on the benefits for the students. Think about what will work for you and read over the ideas given here, and then decide which one you will try. Give yourself permission to be chickenhearted. Just don't be fainthearted!

Some solutions that can help you get started:

- Working with one small group, and a whole-class group with the remaining students, eventually breaking students into smaller groups.

- Work with three groups, but begin by using the same book and scaffolding the lesson. Once you feel comfortable juggling the groups and the students understand the independent time rules, it is time to start differentiating groups through leveled readers.

- Use whole-class reading and follow up. Work with one group in a new book as the other students do reading response in their work area.

- Practice independent work time or center time without meeting with any reading groups. Conduct whole-class reading lessons and use reader response as seat work. If you are using centers, begin with one group at the centers and two groups doing independent work. The goal is to get students to understand expectations of independent work and center time.

Dear Nancy,

I was so gung-ho when I started guided reading. I was one of the teachers who told my principal we needed guided reading. My professors in college drilled into me that students should read on their instructional level. If we teach whole-class reading all the time then some kids are on their independent level, some instructional, and some frustrational all year long. I was psyched because the principal said I could try it. When I finally started and put my students into three groups, it didn't work! No matter what I try, nothing seems to fix the craziness. I feel like my students are all over the place. I mean literally. They interrupt my reading groups to tattle, students walk around when they should be doing their work, and then I find their work is not done. What do I do?

Terrible Teacher from Nowhere

Dear Terrific Teacher Going Places,

Please don't call yourself a terrible teacher! I give you kudos for plunging in.

Now, we need to install a few speed bumps because you are probably driving too fast! I suggest you do a combination of any of the following.

- In a class meeting discuss the rules of guided reading. Explain that each groups gets "their" time and it is not to be interrupted. Students understand the concept of fair. Be fair to all groups; do not interrupt unless it is an emergency.

- Think about your guided reading group time. Are you ending in about twenty to twenty-five minutes? If you are trying to get through "one more thing," twenty minutes can become forty, causing problems.

- In the small reading groups, dedicate some time to finding out what is going on in the classroom while you are working with other groups. In a small-group format all ages are usually more open, and the students might offer you some good insight.

- If your students are young, use a concrete symbol. Some teachers wear a hat or an apron while meeting with small groups. The hat or apron represents "work time" and the group is not to be interrupted.

Dear Nancy,

I have been doing guided reading for a couple of years now and thought I had all the kinks ironed out. But, this year's class has me stymied. Many of my students do not get their reading responses done! I have four groups going at this time, and I can't even pinpoint a group, but out of the twenty-four students in my fourth-grade class, sometimes as many as half have not completed the daily tasks I expect them to do. I know they can because my classes in the past two years were able to do this.

Sincerely,

Queen of Incompletes

Dear Queen,

You don't mention any disruptive behaviors, so I assume that students are in their work areas and working, but work is not getting done. I can't help but wonder if you are seeing this problem in other subjects, such as math? Most likely the answer is yes to that question. My answer is based on thinking that the students must be doing what they get done correctly. Chances are this class is different from your last two years' classes in more ways than this. So, you must deal with them differently. Here are some ideas to help.

- Think of the work tasks as weekly and not daily tasks. Have students keep a work folder for the week, and do not assign any new responses on Friday. Let those who need to "catch up." Let the others have some extra free reading time.

■ Give yourself time between reading groups. Go around and check on the work progress. By now you know who needs the most encouragement, and you should focus on them.

■ Try giving less independent work and more partner work where students are learning through oral interaction, since a lot of writing may be causing some of this problem.

■ Think over the responses and tasks you are assigning. Is there a shorter response you could give that meets the same outcome? If so, change it.

Dear Nancy,

My students constantly interrupt my reading groups to ask questions about their independent work. I think I'm doing things right. I explain, I model, and we do an exercise or two together. I am trying to follow the gradual release of responsibility model, but they still interrupt group time to ask me what to do.

Sincerely,

Sinking in Seattle

Dear Sinking,

I think you need a lift! Because students are interrupting your groups to ask questions about their work, we must assume they want to get their work done. They just cannot for some reason. Hopefully one of the following ideas will be a life preserver for you.

■ Don't meet with guided groups for a few days. Use whole-class reading for a few days. See if students still ask you lots of questions. Assuming they will, take the time to ask what confused them. What did they need to make the tasks clearer to them? Add their suggestions to your next day's teaching.

■ The old motto: "Try three then ask me." If they have asked three others for help and still can't figure out what is to be done, then they may approach you by "signing in" by simply writing their name on the chalkboard or whiteboard. Between reading groups go to the students who have signed up. (Expect this to be overused at first, but the novelty wears off!)

■ Although reading group disruptions are extremely discouraged, sometimes they are necessary (always, of course, with emergencies). If you hear a lot of confusing chatter over work, simply ask what's wrong. A two-minute interruption may give you and the group you are meeting with the next ten in peace.

Dear Nancy,

I prefer to give my students daily responses instead of long-term projects, but I find that some of the students get the work done so quickly, while others take more than the time I think they should. I keep bobbling back and forth. I give them less work and find they have too much time on their hands. Then I give them more work and too many don't finish. Then I give them less work, and too many are done early. . . . It is important to me to have my students working on what is relevant to what they are reading that day. I usually give each group a journal response, some skills work, and some silent or partner reading. What do you suggest?

Bobble Head

Dear Bobble Head,

You have me wobbling just reading this one! It appears that your students are responsibly handling their work, but at a great range of rates. It seems that some of your students need to be challenged more. Try bobbling between these ideas:

■ Consider giving book talks in your classroom to encourage more independent reading. Sometimes teachers feel that if they are not assigning work, the students are not learning. As long as students are engaged in just right leveled books they are increasing their vocabulary, sharpening comprehension skills, and building fluency—let them read!

■ If the students who do not complete their work when you assign a greater amount *are* really working, consider allowing them to do less than the others in their group. For instance, you may ask the students to respond in their journals to the question: "Would you have handled the main character's problem differently? Explain why or why not." For students who have more time add: "If you were a character in the story, what would you have done to help or hinder the main character?"

■ Reconsider staying with just the daily topics. Long-term projects are valuable and can stay current with your daily curriculum expectations. It depends on how you view the project. One suggestion is to have students create their own "Famous Quotations Book Compiled by (Student's Name)." Students collect quotes from books and texts they are reading. The quotes must be copied, cited, and categorized into the proper chapter, such as quotes on: friendship, fairness, or family. Make the categories more complex for older students by adding such categories as growing up, change, or decision making.

■ Consider putting students who finish their work earlier into a short-session literature circle. This will not only enhance the discussion about the text but might also motivate some of the other students to work faster.

Dear Nancy,

My students are really good about getting their center work completed, but they always leave the centers a mess. I do have class rules posted and have talked endlessly about this. It seems I spend twenty to thirty minutes each day just organizing the centers. I am about to

De-center-ize in Despair

Dear De,

I am "center-tive" to your problem. If I were spending two or more hours a week cleaning up after the students I'd be giving up too. Let's talk about organization and expectations. Could it be that you need to have things too neat? I need you to describe *mess* for me. We can accept organized chaos. But here are some ideas that can help students in keeping centers orderly.

■ "A place for everything, and everything in its place" solves most center mess problems. Do you have this? If so, try putting an icon where students are to replace things to remind them where they go.

■ If it is cut papers and scraps on the floor that is bothering you, put a trashcan under the tables where this problem occurs. At the end of the day have a student collect the smaller trashcans and dump them into the school's larger one. I would tell my students they could leave for home after picking up three pieces of trash off the floor!

■ Laminate a list of center close-up steps for *each* center. Students would then use a dry erase marker to check off and sign the cleanup to-do list. This way each student would be held accountable.

Dear Nancy,

I'm not using centers in my room, but long-term projects. What I find is that it takes some students twice as long as others to complete a project. I don't know what to do with the students who have to wait for the next project to begin. I'm afraid that if I start another long-term project the students who are still finishing the first one will get confused. I'm about to give up, but the students create such great projects when we do long-term. Call me . . .

Beaten

Dear Beaten,

What you are describing is very common; don't beat yourself up over this! Try some of these solutions and we'll put the beat back into your long-term projects.

- Consider adding a parallel long-term class project. For instance, let's say you have three guided reading groups in your classroom, and you are doing an author's study. All students are reading a book by Judy Blume. For their individual long-term projects, students are creating accordion books in which they are writing a story that has a similar problem as the Judy Blume book. Some students would finish this in two weeks, others in four depending on the seriousness of their artistry. For a parallel long-term class project, a mural depicting Judy Blume's books and her biography would be a great addition. You can use the mural to teach literary elements, such as setting, by having students only add to the mural settings from the book they are reading. In essence, you end up with a class "Judy Blume setting mural."

- Differentiate your long-term project by assigning a weighted project where students have to do so much of the assigned, but in this case, they must do more if they have time.

- Consider adding optional pieces to what you are doing now. If students are making an ABC book on a topic, give additional options like making a glossary or including a summary page to end the book using all the letter representations. An ABC book on transportation could have the ending: A is for airplane, B is for bus, C is for car . . . Z is for Zodiac.

Dear Nancy,

I have three reading groups in my class, but I have a couple of students that just don't fit. Justin is a little ahead of my lowest group but not able to keep up with the next highest. Then I have Katie who really is a higher level than my middle group, but she's so shy in the higher-level group that she gets "shadowed" by the others. I don't feel I can give them individual reading and I can't make two more groups. I'm not sure what to do.

Concerned

Dear Concerned,

What a wonderful teacher you are! It is obvious that you care about your students' progress and are using your assessments to guide instruction. I must admit my own bias; when a teacher feels a child is in between group levels, I suggest the child be put up into the higher-level group and initially supported to be successful. Here are some suggestions that might help with your concern.

■ Consider forming a fourth group, if it is feasible. Put Justin into the next highest group, and keep the students closer to his level with him. Put Katie and other strong readers from her original group into a second highest group level, mixing these students with some slightly weaker ones from the top group. Having four groups will make the groups smaller, and this smaller group size may help Katie feel more comfortable. Keep in mind that groups should be flexible. This arrangement would work until you realize some others have gotten too strong for their group!

■ Place Justin and Katie in two groups. Have them work with the group you now have them placed in, but have them join the discussion and part of the assigned responses in the higher group. Eventually Justin will catch up. In Katie's case, she will most likely grow more comfortable.

■ If the concern with Katie is her shyness, have her meet with the top group a couple of times a week until she is comfortable. In Justin's case, put him in the next level group and partner him with a strong reader for a few weeks. Let them do all their work and reading together. This will scaffold Justin's learning, allows his partner some deserved pride, and does not take away from the time you need with the reading groups.

In Conclusion

My unsolicited advice: Begin a study group within your school. Meet once a week and bring breakfast. Talk about the problems that you are having; most likely others have had or are still experiencing the same problem. If someone hasn't solved the problem yet, brainstorm ideas together. Teachers enjoy study groups and they help make what can be an isolated profession more social. They feel they are listened to and that they learn a great deal from others. The study group becomes a support group and everyone, especially the students, wins.

CHAPTER 14

Putting It All Together

This chapter sends us into the classroom of Amy Bard. Amy has twenty-two children in her third-grade urban classroom. She has paraprofessional help but unfortunately only in the afternoon. This is an advantage because when Amy notices a student is not "catching on" or misunderstanding concepts, Amy has the paraprofessional work with the student (or students) for a short period of time.

To form three reading groups Amy used the results of an informal reading inventory (IRI), a "quick check," and a schoolwide reading test to group her students. Although some teachers simply group their students by the schoolwide reading test, Amy wants to be certain of her students' levels. Amy does her very informal quick check to confirm the results. Because Amy's students are in grade 3, she does not feel she has to do a formal running record with all her children. She will do running records with those who are below grade 3 reading level to guide her in decisions for phonics and word attack instruction for that group.

The quick check is simple for Amy. She looks at the results of the IRI and the schoolwide reading assessment to see what level the child is near and chooses a book near that level. Amy then has each child read to her orally during the students' free reading time or when she can "grab" a student as others work. This usually takes Amy two to three days. She does not do a miscue analysis at this time, because most students will not make enough miscues to analyze as she is already in the ballpark of their instructional level.

The independent, instructional (just right), and frustration levels are calculated as in a running record, by counting errors. Self-corrections are not errors, but omitting words and substituting words are errors. Amy is simply counting on her fingers the number of words students read incorrectly or omit. She is looking for percentages of words correct . She knows that 95 to 100 percent is the independent level, 90 to 94 percent is the instructional level, and anything below is frustrational. Amy is using the quick check as a third indicator for placement. These groups will change through the year. Amy knows that some students learn faster than others; some will have come into a developmental cycle where they are ready to fly. Now she needs a beginning placement. For those students near third-grade level or higher, Amy has them read at least 100 words from a grade 3–level book. She has a light marking after the one hundredth word, so she will stop counting with her fingers and let the student continue reading until they have finished a short but meaningful passage. With one hundred words, Amy knows that if she runs out of fingers . . . well, the grade 3 book is at the frustration level for this student (below 90 percent). She will try an easier book later with this child. For students near the grade 2 level, Amy has a grade 2–level book, in which she has a light mark near the fiftieth word. She chooses fifty words for these students because they often read slower. She listens to the child read and ticks off on her fingers; if she gets past one hand, she knows the student is already under the 90 percent. With grade 1 readers, Amy also stops ticking at fifty words using a grade 1–level book.

For example, Juan scored grade 2 on the IRI but grade 1 on the school-wide assessment. Amy feels Juan is capable, but because English is his second language, he struggles to show what he can do. Amy chooses to have Juan read the level-one book, and she ticks off three errors (out of the fifty words), and she feels that Juan read at a reasonable rate and with expression. She knows, at 94 percent correct, that this text is at Juan's instructional level. But because his rate and expression showed strength and based on the grade 2 level on the IRI, Amy has decided to also try Juan in the grade 2–level book. As Juan reads, Amy ticks off four errors, which puts Juan at 92 percent in this reading of the fifty words. When in doubt, Amy places the child at the higher level. Based on the results of all three assessments, and her own professional judgment of how Juan's reading sounds, Amy will initially place Juan in the grade 2–level book. Amy jots down the results and this has taken Amy less than four minutes. For most students the quick test will take two to three minutes from start to finish, even less if the quick test simply supports the other assessments.

Sometimes the support is not there. When this occurs, Amy using professional judgment, places the child at where at least two assessments have the child, and notes that things may be different.

Amy looks at her whole class profile. Comfortable with three groups, she looks at the levels of the students and decides on one low second-grade level (around J on Fountas and Pinnell scale), one group in beginning grade 3 (Fountas and Pinnell scale, around level N), and one ending grade 3 (Fountas and Pinnell scale, around level P) (Fountas and Pinnell 2001).

Timewise Amy can give a ten-minute minilesson daily, meet with the two lower groups for twenty-five minutes daily, and the higher group for twenty. She has purposely built in "free" segments of five minutes in the daily schedule. Amy knows if she gets a little behind, she can catch up with the built-in time and her plan is to check on progress and problems between group meetings.

The following weeklong scenario gives a picture of how Amy's classroom looks in action. The project for the week is a four-page (fold) accordion display for haiku the children are writing; they will write four haiku. Amy read the book *Haiku Hike* (Fourth Grade Students 2005), which is a book of haiku written by fourth-grade students who had gone on a nature hike. This delightful book has information about nature, along with the haiku. The book also explains the syllabication rules of haiku and that each haiku is to have a "kigo" included, which is a seasonal word or phrase. Being in an urban district, Amy gave students pictures of nature and natural settings.

Amy has prepared accordion folded paper. On the thick paper students will illustrate and write their haiku for final draft. Amy is planning to display the finished products in the children's section of the public library. She knows her students would love that, and it will motivate them to perfection! When students have done what is assigned for their project that day, they get additional free reading time. They understand they are to read and not disrupt others.

The reading group on grade 2 level is reading *Keep the Lights Burning, Abbie* (Roop and Roop 1985). This delightful book is based on a true story about a family living at a lighthouse on Matinicus Rock near the coast of Maine. Abbie's father had to sail to the mainland for supplies and medicine for Abbie's sick mother. Due to tremendous storms, he could not return for weeks. Abbie kept the lighthouse lights burning and the ships safe at sea.

The beginning grade 3 group is reading *Keeker and the Sneaky Pony* (Higginson 2006). This book focuses on a young girl, Keeker, who gets her much-wanted pony, Plum. Keeker is stranded on her first ride when on purpose Plum "bucks" Keeker to the ground. Plum never wanted a girl, anyway. Keeker eventually finds Plum, scratches her back, and pony and owner become friends.

The grade 3 group that is nearing grade 4 level is reading *The Girl with 500 Middle Names* (Haddix 2001). In this book, Janie's parents move from a poor urban area to the suburbs so Janie, a third grader, can attend a better school. Janie's mother, who had been making extra money selling specialty name sweaters, gets swindled and loses money. Janie, in support of her parents' plight, wears sweaters with other people's names. The book focuses on Janie's difficulty being poor in a rich school and her family's struggles.

Figure 14-1. *Weekly Plan*

Monday

8:45–8:55 Whole-Class Minilesson
Focus: Project for week
Explanation of accordion display. Tell children about the project that should be finished by Friday. Show accordion folded paper; explain one haiku will go on each "page" in between folds. They may choose a season for their haiku when picking pictures. Review criteria for haiku; write one together. Their task today is to write two haiku on draft paper. Have a partner check the number of syllables with them.

Note: Follow group work down the column.

Time	Grade 2–Level Group	Beginning Grade 3–Level Group	Ending Grade 3–Level Group
9:00–9:25	**Teacher Time** Read to children "A note from Author," which gives real background. Predict from this and cover. Guide students through to page 10 (father leaves and the responsibility of the light is left to Abbie).	**Project Time** Explained in minilesson.	**Independent Work Time** In preparation for book. Journal response: Write what you would like in a new school if you had to move. What would your new best friend be like?
9:30–9:55	**Independent Work Time** Reread the text at your seat. Respond in journal to the question: Why do Abbie's legs feel "too heavy to run?"	**Teacher Time** Story introduction: Build background on ponies, care, etc. Introduce book and have students do a picture walk.	**Project Time** Explained in minilesson.
10:00–10:20	**Project Time** Explained in minilesson.	**Independent Work Time** With partners students read information on ponies (pony facts) at the end of the book (three pages). Write down five new things you learned about ponies.	**Teacher Time** Introduce book. Read first page to students. Build background on urban and suburban areas. Show a picture of a large spread-out suburban school and a three- or four-story urban school. Discuss differences.

Figure 14–1. *continued*

Tuesday

| 8:45–8:55 Whole-Class Minilesson
Focus: Review haiku
Discuss and share a couple of haiku from yesterday. Give directions for illustrations: topic must be taken from haiku, and the drawings must cover the complete "page." Drawings will be done with light-colored markers. They need to consider one area where they will actually write their haiku. When ready the haiku will be written with black marker. Assign two illustrations today. Also, do a neat second draft of haiku. Remember three lines of five, seven, and five syllables. |

Time	Grade 2–Level Group	Beginning Grade 3–Level Group	Ending Grade 3–Level Group
9:00–9:25	**Teacher Time** Read to page 18 (Abbie's father leaves). Guide the reading. Discuss author's voice, use of verbs: wind carried voice out, Puffin (the boat) slides out to sea, page 14 simile "as high as the sky."	**Project Time** Explained in minilesson.	**Independent Work Time** On a prediction chart predict what will happen (remember what happened on the first page). Using the list of names given, write five sets of first and middle names. Explain why you think these names go together.
9:30–9:55	**Independent Work Time** Students will watch the background-building part of the Reading Rainbow tape of this book (about ten minutes). Journal response: Write about a responsibility you would not like to have and explain why.	**Teacher Time** Guided reading, Chapter 1. Read first page and discuss using third person. Discuss the two characters' perspective: Plum (doesn't want a girl) and Keeker, who wants a pony.	**Project Time** Explained in minilesson.
10:00–10:20	**Project Time** Explained in minilesson.	**Independent Work Time** Given "thought balloon paper" write in the thought balloons the thoughts or perceived thoughts of Keeker and Plum. Skim the chapter for ideas.	**Teacher Time** Build background on "cross-eyed." Discuss foreshadowing and the first lines in the book. Guide students through Chapter 1. Discuss: Why did Krissy say, "You're lying"?

Figure 14–1. *continued*

Wednesday

8:45 to 8:55 Whole-Class Minilesson
Focus: Haiku writing
Show two haiku models from literature on the overhead. Compare good points with two of Monday's drafts. Write the second two haiku for the last two accordion pages. Discuss good ideas seen in yesterday's illustrations.

Time	Grade 2–Level Group	Beginning Grade 3–Level Group	Ending Grade 3–Level Group
9:00–9:25	**Teacher Time** Guided reading pages 20-26 (Abbie lights lamps and saves ship at sea). Show students pictures of old lighthouse lamps and explain how they use oil and wicks.	**Project Time** Explained in minilesson.	**Independent Work Time** Fill in what happened on the prediction chart. Predict for Chapter 2. With a partner do a readers' theatre on Chapter 1.
9:30–9:55	**Independent Work Time** Reread with partners page 26. In a four-square sequence (paper to be given), students draw and write how Abbie was able to light the match (got matches, match went out, light another match, held near wick).	**Teacher Time** Guided reading for Chapter 2. Discuss questions: (1)Why did Keeker say Plum was sneaky? (2) Was it right for Keeker to have a temper trantrum? Explain.	**Project Time** Explained in minilesson.
10:00–10:20	**Project Time** Explained in minilesson.	**Independent Work Time** With a partner reread Chapter 2. Use a Venn diagram to compare the father's approach to Keeker's approach to the pony.	**Teacher Time** Guided reading for Chapter 2. Discuss multiple meanings of magic. Compare how wonderful your school is to the one described in the book. Discuss the tactics Mom used to get Dad to move.

Figure 14–1. *continued*

Thursday

8:45–8:55 Whole-Class Minilesson
Focus: Haiku drafting and illustrations
Repeat with class what is needed from Tuesday's lesson. They are to draw the last two illustrations and fix yesterday's haiku. They may write in pencil the first haiku on the accordion pages. They are to make a clean draft of the last two haiku to be checked.

Time	Grade 2–Level Group	Beginning Grade 3–Level Group	Ending Grade 3–Level Group
9:00–9:25	**Teacher Time** Guided reading of pages 28 to 35. Discuss how the author uses suspense in this section.	**Project Time** Explained in minilesson.	**Independent Work Time** Reread Chapter 2 with a partner. Think of something that both of you want. Write a plan including the "tactics" you could use to get what you want. Fill in what happened in Chapter 2, predict Chapter 3.
9:30–9:55	**Independent Work Time** Students independently reread pages 28 to 35. On graphic organizer describe three "close calls" in this chapter (the hens, Abbie racing, shutting the door).	**Teacher Time** Make predictions, then guided reading for Chapter 3. Discuss author's use of sound effects to show speed (clippety clop, swish-swosh). On page 26, what does the author mean by "The whole forest seemed to be moving"?	**Project Time** Explained in minilesson.
10:00–10:20	**Project Time** Explained in minilesson.	**Independent Work Time** Journal response: Tell about a time you did something that your parents did not want you to do. Add some sound effects in the description.	**Teacher Time** Semantic web going to a new school and making new friends. Guided reading of Chapter 3. Discussion web: Was Janie's first day at school good or bad? What things are more important than money?

Figure 14–1. *continued*

Friday

8:45–8:55 Whole-Class Minilesson
Focus: Project completion
Write the last two haiku in pencil. Because the first two haiku have been checked, write over the pencil in black marker. Write in the last two in pencil. Check these before they use marker. Because we are publishing for display, we want it perfect. I will put a little extra time in between groups today. One group will finish theirs on Monday during their project time.

Time	Grade 2–Level Group	Beginning Grade 3–Level Group	Ending Grade 3–Level Group
9:00–9:25	**Teacher Time** Guided reading of pages 36–40. Predict. On page 36 discuss how the author uses repetition to show mood, discuss whether Abbie was a heroine, and support with text.	**Project Time** Explained in minilesson.	**Independent Work Time** Read Chapter 4 independently (partner J & N). Think about the children at the new school. Who was nice, who wasn't? On your prediction chart write what happened in Chapters 3 and 4. Predict for Chapter 5.
9:30–9:55	**Independent Work Time** Partners fill out story map. Write in the main problem but on the back of the paper write other problems that Abbie faced. Be prepared to discuss in the group.	**Teacher Time** Share sound effects and meaning from journal. Make predictions, then guided reading of Chapter 4. Do a discussion web with the question: Is it Keeker's fault she is lost? Yes or no?	**Project Time** Explained in minilesson.
10:00–10:20	**Project Time** Explained in minilesson.	**Independent Work Time** Draw a picture of Keeker "doing her thing." Around the picture write all the things she could be thinking about in this chapter.	**Teacher Time** Discuss opinions—who was nice/not nice at the new school. Guide students in Chapter 5. Discuss the "awkward moment" in the text, share connections.

Before and After This Week's Lessons

For this week's minilessons Amy chose to do the accordion display and to focus on haiku. Last week Amy focused on syllabication, hearing sounds and dividing words to aid the students in the creation of haiku. Amy noticed that students struggled with descriptive vocabulary in their haiku. The students' language was not as colorful as she had hoped, although she was very happy with the haiku. She will focus at least three of next week's minilessons on descriptive vocabulary and ask students to find unusual descriptive vocabulary in their reading. They will continue with their books during their guided reading groups.

In Conclusion

Guided reading is so much more than guiding students through a text. The peripherals of guided reading make the challenge and the joy. The area supporting the guided reading context is one that allows so much creativity as students are supported through important facets of the curriculum. It does take time, but seeing student creations and getting to know your students in small groups bring such joy. The teachers, like you, who do this and do this well, insist it is worth all the time and effort. Enjoy your journey!

Allington, R. 2001. *What Really Matters for Struggling Readers: Designing Research-Based Programs.* New York: Longman.

Armbruster, B., F. Lehr, and J. Osborne. 2001. *Put Reading First: The Research Building Blocks for Teaching Children to Read.* Partnership for Reading. U.S. Department of Education Publication.

Barton, J., and M. Sawyer. 2004. "Our Students Are Ready for This: Comprehension Instruction in the Elementary Classroom." *The Reading Teacher,* December 2003, January 2004, Newark, New Jersey: International Reading Association. 57: 334–49.

Beck, I., M. McKeown, and L. Kucan. 2002. *Bringing Words to Life: Robust Vocabulary Instruction.* New York: Guilford.

Braunger, J., and J. P. Lewis. 2006. *Building a Knowledge Base in Reading, 2nd ed.* Newark, NJ: International Reading Association and The National Council of Teachers of English.

Buehl, D. 2001. *Classroom Strategies for Interactive Learning.* Newark, NJ: International Reading Association.

Caldwell, A. S. and L. Leslie. 2005. *Intervention Strategies to Follow Informal Reading Inventory Assessment.* Boston: Pearson.

Cooper, J. D. 2001. *Literacy: Helping Children Construct Meaning.* New York: Houghton Mifflin.

Cunningham, P. 2005. *Phonics They Use, 4th ed.* Boston: Pearson.

Devine, T. 1987. *Teaching Study Skills: A Guide for Teachers, 2nd ed.* Boston: Allyn and Bacon.

Diller, D. 2003. *Literacy Work Stations: Making Centers Work.* Portland, ME: Stenhouse.

Farris, P., C. Fuhler, and M. Walther. 2004. *Teaching Reading: A Balanced Approach for Today's Classrooms.* New York: McGraw Hill.

Fountas, I. and S. G. Pinnell. 1996. *Guided Reading: Good First Teaching for All Children.* Portsmouth, NH: Heinemann.

———. 2001. *Guiding Readers and Writers Grades 3–6.* Portsmouth, NH: Heinemann.

Graves, M. 2006. *The Vocabulary Book.* Newark, NJ: IRA, Teachers College Press, and NCTE.

Harvey, S. and A. Goudvis. 2000. *Strategies That Work*. Portland, ME: Stenhouse.

Jennings, J. H., J. Caldwell, and J. W. Lerner. 2006. *Reading Problems: Assessment and Teaching Strategies, 5th ed.* Boston: Pearson.

Keene, E. O., and S. Zimmermann. 1997. *Mosaic of Thought*. Portsmouth, NH: Heinemann.

Manzo, A., U. Manzo, and T. Estes. 2000. *Content Area Literacy: Interactive Teaching for Active Learning, 3rd ed.* San Francisco: John Wiley & Sons.

McCardle, P. and V. Chhabra. 2004. *The Voice of Evidence in Reading Research*. Baltimore: Paul H. Brookes.

McEwan, E. 2004. *Seven Strategies of Highly Effective Readers*. Thousand Oaks, CA: Corwin.

Moore, D. W., S. A. Moore, P. M. Cunningham, and J. W. Cunningham. 2003. *Developing Readers and Writers in the Content Areas K–12, 4th ed.* New York: Longman.

Nettles, D. 2006. *Toolkit for Teachers of Literacy*. Boston: Allyn and Bacon.

Owocki, G. 2005. *Time for Literacy Centers: How to Organize and Differentiate Instruction*. Portsmouth, NH: Heinemann.

Pearson, D., and M. Gallagher. "The Instruction of Reading Comprehension." *Contemporary Educational Psychology* 8, 1983.

Prescott-Griffin, M., and N. L. Witherell. 2004. *Fluency in Focus: Comprehension Strategies for All Young Readers*. Portsmouth, NH: Heinemann.

Roberts, P. L., R. D. Kellough, and K. Moore. 2006. *A Resource Guide for Elementary School Teaching: Planning for Competence, 6th ed.* Upper Saddle River, NJ: Pearson, Merrill Prentice Hall.

Tyner, B., and S. Green. 2005. *Small-Group Reading Instruction: A Differentiated Teaching Model for Intermediate Readers, Grades 3–8*. Newark, DE: International Reading Association.

Vardell, S., N. Hadaway, and T. Young. 2006. "Matching Books and Readers: Selecting Literatures for English Learners." *The Reading Teacher* 59 (8): 734–41.

Vaughn, S., and S. Linan-Thompson. 2004. *Research-Based Methods of Reading Instruction K–3*. Alexandria, VA: ASCD.

Vygotsky, L. S. 1978. *Mind in Society: The Development of Higher Psychological Processes*. Cole, M., V. John-Steiner, S. Scribner, and E. Souberman, eds. and trans. Cambridge, MA: Harvard University Press (original work published in 1934).

Witherell, N. 2000. "Promoting Understanding: Teaching Literacy through the Arts." *Educational Horizons* (Summer 2000). Pi Lambda Theta Publication.

Witherell, N. L. 1995. *Vocabulary Matters*. Unpublished Paper. Massachusetts Reading Association Annual Conference.

Witherell, N. L. and M. C. McMackin. 2002. *Graphic Organizers and Activities for Differentiated Instruction in Reading*. New York: Scholastic.

Children's Books

Ahlberg, J., and A. Ahlberg. 1986. *The Jolly Postman or Other People's Letters*. Boston: Little Brown.

Armstrong, W. 1969. *Sounder*. New York: HarperCollins.

Baillie, A. 1992. *Little Brother*. New York: Penguin.

Bang, M. 1983. *Ten, Nine, Eight.* New York: Scholastic.

Barracca D. and S. Barracca. 1990. *The Adventures of Taxi Dog.* New York: Trumpet.

Blume, J. 1980. *Superfudge.* New York: Dell.

Brown, M. 1994. *Arthur's Chicken Pox.* Boston: Little, Brown.

Carle, E. 1987. *Have You Seen My Cat?* Saxonville, MA: Picture Book Studio.

Cleary, B. 1965. *The Mouse and the Motorcycle.* New York: HarperCollins.

———. 1981. *Dear Mr. Henshaw.* New York: HarperCollins.

Clifton, Lucille. 1976. *Three Wishes.* New York: Viking.

Cole, J. 1969. *The Magic School Bus Inside the Human Body.* New York: Scholastic.

Cooney, B. 1994. *Only Opal, The Diary of a Young Girl.* New York: Scholastic.

Cronin, D. 2000. *Click, Clack, Moo Cows That Type.* New York: Simon and Schuster for Young Readers.

———. 2003. *Diary of a Worm.* New York: Scholastic.

Curtis, C. P. 1999. *Bud, Not Buddy.* New York: Scholastic.

Da Costa Nunez, R., and J. A. Ellison. 2005. *Voyage to Shelter Cove.* New York: White Tiger Press.

Dahl, R. 1981. *George's Marvelous Medicine.* New York: Penguin.

Day, A. 1986. *Good Dog, Carl.* New York: Simon and Schuster.

Elting, M. and M. Folsom. 1980. *Q is for Duck: An Alphabet Guessing Game.* New York: Clarion.

Flor Ada, A. 2001. *With Love, Little Red Hen.* New York: Atheneum.

Flournoy, V. 1985. *The Patchwork Quilt.* New York: Scholastic.

Fourth Grade Students of St. Mary's Catholic School in Mansfield, Massachusetts. 2005. *Haiku Hike.* New York: Scholastic.

Gantos, J. 2000. *Joey Pigza Loses Control.* New York: Scholastic.

Haddix, M. P. 2001. *The Girl with 500 Middle Names.* New York: Aladdin Paperbacks.

Hansen, J. 1986. *Yellow Bird and Me.* New York: Clarion.

Hicyilmaz, G. 1990. *Against the Storm.* New York: Yearling, Dell.

Higginson, H. 2006. *Keeker and the Sneaky Pony.* San Francisco: Chronicle.

Hobbs, W. 1996. *Far North.* New York: HarperCollins.

Howard, E. F. 1991. *Aunt Flossie's Hats (and Crab Cakes Later).* New York: Clarion.

Hurst, C. O. 2001. *Rocks in His Head.* New York: HarperCollins.

Keats, E. J. 1962. *The Snowy Day.* New York: Viking.

———. 1964. *Peter's Chair.* New York: Harper Collins.

Konigsburg, E. L. 1996. *A View from Saturday.* New York: Aladdin Paperbacks.

———. 2001. *Jennifer, Hecate, Macbeth, William McKinley, and Me, Elizabeth.* New York: Aladdin Paperbacks.

Koontz, R. M. 2000. *Why a Dog? By A. Cat.* New York: Scholastic.

London, J. 1992. *Froggy Gets Dressed.* New York: Scholastic.

Lord, B. B. 1984. *In the Year of the Boar and Jackie Robinson.* New York: HarperCollins.

Lowry, L. 1990. *Number the Stars.* New York: Scholastic.

MacLachlan, P. 1985. *Sarah, Plain and Tall.* New York: Scholastic.

Martin, B. 1983. *Brown Bear, Brown Bear, What Do You See?* New York: Henry Holt.

McKissack, P. 1986. *Flossie and the Fox.* New York: Scholastic.

Mitchell, M. K. 1993. *Uncle Jed's Barbershop*. New York: Simon and Schuster Books for Young Readers.

Naylor, P. R. 1992. *Josie's Troubles*. New York: Yearling.

———. 2000. *Shiloh*. New York: Aladdin Paperbacks.

Palatini, M. 2003. *The Perfect Pet*. New York: HarperCollins.

Pallotta, J. 2000. *The Icky Bug Alphabet Book*. Watertown, MA: Charlesbridge.

Parish, H. 1999. *Amelia Bedelia 4 Mayor*. New York: Scholastic.

Patneaude, D. 1993. *Someone Was Watching*. Morton Grove, IL: Albert Whitman.

Pellegrini, N. 1991. *Families Are Different*. New York: Scholastic.

Pottle, R. 2005. *Moxie Day, The Prankster: Another Laugh and Learn Book of Poetry*. Eastbrook, ME: Blue Lobster Press.

Ray, D. K. 1990. *My Daddy Was a Soldier*. New York: Holiday House.

Ritter, J. H. 2000. *Over the Wall*. New York: Puffin.

Rohmann, E. 2002. *My Friend Rabbit*. New York: Scholastic.

Roop, P. and C. Roop. 1985. *Keep the Lights Burning, Abbie*. Minneapolis, MN: Carolrhoda.

Rossiter, R. 1994. *The Greedy Man in the Moon*. Petersburg, FL: Riverbank.

Sachar, L. 1998. *Holes*. New York: Yearling.

Schotter, R. 2003. *In the Piney Woods*. New York: Farrar, Straus and Giroux.

Scott, A. H. 1972. *On Mother's Lap*. New York: Scholastic.

Slobodkina, E. 1968. *Caps for Sale*. New York: HarperTrophy.

Snicket, Lemony. 1999–2006. A Series of Unfortunate Events. New York: Scholastic.

Spinelli, E. 2000. *Night Shift Daddy*. New York: Hyperion.

Spinelli, J. 1990. *Maniac Magee*. Boston: Little Brown.

Sykes, J. 1997. *Dora's Eggs*. New York: Scholastic.

Uchida, Y. 1993. *The Bracelet*. New York: Putnam & Grosset Group.

Viorst, J. 1980. *Alexandra Who Used to Be Rich Last Sunday*. New York: Aladdin.

Waber, B. 1972. *Ira Sleeps Over*. Boston: Houghton Mifflin.

Walsh, E. S. 1989. *Mouse Paint*. New York: Trumpet.

Wang, R. 1991. *The Fourth Question: A Chinese Tale*. New York: Bantam, Doubleday, Dell.

White, E. B. 1952. *Charlotte's Web*. New York: HarperCollins.

Wilder, L. I. 1935. *Little House on the Prairie*. New York: Avon.

Williams, V. 1982. *A Chair for My Mother*. New York: Scholastic.